Counting
the Rivers

Pearlie McNeill began writing
autobiographical pieces in 1975, and in
1989 published *One of the Family*, which
was highly commended in the 1990
Australian Human Rights Awards. She lives
in Woonona, New South Wales.

Counting the Rivers is the inaugural
winner of the Wirra Wirra/Wakefield Press
Award for Unpublished Non-fiction.

by the same author

One of the Family

Women's Voices, Refugee Lives edited with Meg Coulson

Women Talk Sex edited with Bea Freeman and Jenny Newman

Through the Break edited with Pratibha Parmar and Marie McShea

And So Say All of Us edited with Marie McShea

Counting the Rivers

Pearlie McNeill

Wakefield Press

Wakefield Press
Box 2266
Kent Town
South Australia 5071

First published 1998

Edited by Jenny Lee
Designed by Liz Nicholson and Nick Stewart, design BITE, Adelaide
Cover photograph *Blue Tights*, c type photo by Deborah Paauwe
courtesy Greenaway Art Gallery
Typeset by Clinton Ellicott, MoBros, Adelaide
Printed and bound by Hyde Park Press, Adelaide

National Library of Australia
Cataloguing-in-publication entry

McNeill, Pearlie.
Counting the rivers.

ISBN 1 86254 452 2.

1. Psychotherapy patients – Australia – Biography.
I. Title.

362.2092

Publication of this book was assisted by the Commonwealth Government
through the Australia Council, its arts funding and advisory body.

Wakefield Press thanks Arts SA and Wirra Wirra for their continued
support and for sponsoring the Wirra Wirra/Wakefield Press Award
for Unpublished Non-fiction.

contents

PART

Counting

Stone walls do not a
prison make,
Nor iron bars a cage

FROM RICHARD LOVELACE,
'TO ALTHEA FROM PRISON',
1658

Counting

The knowledge doesn't come quickly, not like switching on a light. This is a slow-dawning awareness. What is happening to her can't be described as a headache or a pain in the back. If only it was that simple. The more Madeleine thinks and worries about it, the more convinced she becomes. Something alien has crawled inside her skin and grown – not an insect or a tiny animal, but some strange machine. There can be no other explanation.

The relentless grinding wakes her early, a gut-sickening clash of gears. Each morning is like waking from a nightmare only to realise that what she's dreamt is horrifyingly real. She imagines her fear as a small lizard, agile and slippery, coursing through her body in a mad panic, alerting the machine that she is frightened. Her older brother taught her never to show fear to a dog, but this is inside her – how can she stay calm?

It takes her ages to walk to the kitchen, even longer to fill the kettle. Her head buzzes with questions. What will become of her? Will she one day lose her mind to this bloody machine?

MENTAL HEALTH ACT (1958) AS AMENDED

SECTION 21 (1) (a)

Form of Application for Admission of a Voluntary Patient

PATIENT'S No. ....

I, __MADELEINE ROBERTS__
(State name in full)

hereby request that I be admitted

*Admission to the * __PARRAMATTA PSYCHIATRIC CENTRE__

Centre,

Mental   for treatment as a voluntary patient, and if admitted I agree to

Hospital or abide by any regulations the Medical Superintendent may lay down

Authorised

Hospital.   on me.

Signature of patient .... __M. Roberts__

I CERTIFY that the above application was made voluntarily,

in my presence, by the above named.

Signature of Witness .... __John Roberts__

Date ....

Relationship (if any) to patient .... __husband__

(This application by the patient should be witnessed by a relative or friend

of the patient or, if this is impracticable, by an officer of the hospital

other than a medical officer.)

ABD841 — W   V.C.N. Blight, Government Printer

The car stops outside the entrance to Ward 60. A nurse is there to meet them. She suggests John leave straight away so that Madeleine can settle in before lunch. John gets out of the car and hurries around to hand Madeleine her bag. He kisses her on the cheek and promises to visit as soon as the doctor gives the OK. Madeleine watches him drive away. A long hissing sound reverberates inside her. She half expects steam to be coming out of her ears. She narrows her eyes till all she can see is the back of the nurse's neck. Put one foot in front of the other. Keep moving. Don't think about anything, anything at all.

Leading the way inside, the nurse explains that Ward 60 is close to the river that runs from Sydney Harbour to Parramatta then further west. Madeleine listens with a measure of comfort. If a river can travel beyond this place, then hopefully so can she.

The last few months have been traumatic. Daily happenings jar her, knock her off balance. Once she would have laughed; now tears stream from her eyes for no apparent reason, everyday activities tax her waning strength. She feels out of tune with life. It's as if she's been thrown onto a conveyor belt, removed at a moment's notice from her familiar life, swept past the rooms of several psychiatrists, gathering files, medical opinions and prescriptions, as she hurtles towards an unpredictable future. No one asks if she'd like to get off this hurdy-gurdy. Each doctor simply presses a button with a sign over it that reads FASTER. Now she is being admitted to one of 'those' hospitals – twenty-eight years old, depressed, disoriented, convinced a machine is taking over her body. Is she mad? Maybe, maybe not. There is definitely something wrong, but does the root of the problem lie in her belly or her mind? Surely someone here will be able to help? What kind of help, though? Would a psychiatrist order an investigation of her insides? Would they tell her it was all in her imagination? And what if they were right? Would she slide into delirium, eyes vacant, mouth slack, thinking gone awry? Questions, so many questions. Mad, but how mad? Nutty as a fruit cake? A lunatic? How does anyone decide?

She follows the nurse through a large high-ceilinged room, allowing herself brief glances left and right. Several tall windows look out onto a grassy patch near the entrance. Smaller windows on the other side reveal a flagstone veranda. Chairs line the walls. In the middle of the room a long wooden coffee table overflows with pamphlets and newspapers. The newspapers have yellowed, and Madeleine can see they are old. Much later she learns that this is the day-room.

In the corridor beyond there are three doors. The nearest is marked STOREROOM in big, black letters. Through the open door Madeleine notices different sorts of medical equipment stored on several deep shelves. A man in a white coat is unloading a supply of tall brown bottles. The next door is also open. She catches a glimpse of tidily made beds. Now she and the nurse are standing in front of the third door.

The door is wide and solid. The nurse knocks loudly. Almost immediately a woman's face peers at them through a small glass panel. The face nods once, then disappears. They hear the sound of a key turning in the lock. Madeleine is reminded of a late-night radio programme she listened to as a child. Each episode began and ended with the opening of a door, its rusty hinges creaking in protest. She remembers the feeling she used to get when she heard that door.

Well, here is another inner sanctum and yes, she is scared. She resolves to stay as tight and still as she possibly can.

The door swings inwards. The face at the window belongs to a nurse. Once Madeleine and her companion step inside, the door is promptly closed and locked. The key is still in the lock. It is one of several held together on a metal ring. A long length of chain connects the metal ring to a clip on the nurse's belt. What if someone very strong and very mad were to come along and rip the door off its hinges? What would happen to the nurse? Worried she might burst into hysterical giggles, Madeleine focuses her attention on the chain, counting the links.

The conversation between the two nurses is brisk and to the point. A clipboard is handed over, and the nurse with the keys signs the top sheet of paper. Madeleine has been delivered and signed for.

She stands at the foot of the nearest bed and continues to count. The hissing in her ears is quieter, but a heavy clanking has started up in the background. Her stomach feels as though it is being pinched by a tight corset. It is always more difficult to breathe when this happens. She is concerned that someone will notice. If she looks around, the other patients will see and know about the machine. She mustn't look, they mustn't see. No one must know – who'd believe her anyway?

Two women are talking in soft whispers near by. Are they discussing her? *A hundred and thirty-three, a hundred and thirty-four, a hundred and thirty-five*. Her eyes go funny the nearer she gets to the key. Damn. She can hardly step closer to do the job properly. She'll have to find something else to count. What about those dirty marks on the floor? Number one is close to her left foot, number two is a rubber scratch mark under one wheel of the bed opposite. What about that ball of fluff scudding across the floor near the door? Would that do for number three? Does fluff count? Not really. Dirt is a definite statement; fluff is mobile, which makes it something else. Before she can find another number three, the key is once more turning in the lock. The guide nurse leaves without looking back.

Madeleine bites her tongue, holding back a strong urge to scream. She is locked up, locked in, alone with these strangers. All the people she knows, her children, her husband, her friends and neighbours, are on the other side of that door. She mustn't dwell on these thoughts – it won't change anything. Better not to think, better to count.

For a brief moment she forgets where she is. Her eyes wander. This is a mistake. Now she *knows* the women are staring at her. She pretends not to notice, makes her eyes go blank, gazes into the middle distance. If she drops her eyes to the floor too quickly they'll know. Forget the dirty marks. She'll count beds instead. There are fourteen along each wall, metal-framed, each with its own coverlet of crisp, white cotton.

The nurse is clipping the bunch of keys on to her belt. Ignoring Madeleine entirely, she walks the length of the ward, but Madeleine is catching on fast. She fights against the clamour in her belly, the nausea rising in her throat. She falls into line, keeping a respectful distance, as the nurse pushes open a swing door.

Inside, the walls are covered in white tiles. The floor is tiled too, a grey-green expanse of tiny squares. The room is large, with a wide space between the shower stalls and the row of vanity basins. A partition separates the showers from the toilets. In an alcove at the other end, a bath juts out from the wall. Alongside the bath is a locked cupboard. The only door is the one leading back into the ward.

The nurse's voice echoes in the room.

'Put your bag by the door, Madeleine, and I'll pack it away. You won't be wearing your own clothes for a while, but if there's anything you need, ask one of the nurses. I want you to undress now and have a bath.'

Madeleine places her bag near the door but makes no move to undress. The noises in her head are bouncing off the walls. Darting pains stab somewhere below her ribs. Oh God, please make it stop, please.

Meanwhile, the nurse sets about running a bath. She pulls the plug on its chain from a dangling position over the spout, drops it into place and turns on both taps. Madeleine locks her attention onto the running water. If she concentrates hard enough, maybe she can drown out the pandemonium.

The nurse's next words are sharp.

'Haven't you started getting undressed yet? Come on, I haven't got all day.'

Madeleine looks around her. There's no chair, no stool, no wall hooks, nothing.

'Where . . . where will I put my clothes?'

'On the floor. Make sure you fold them neatly, though. Now hurry up, it's nearly lunchtime.'

Madeleine unzips her skirt, her fingers fumbling so much she can't get a firm grip. She steps out of the skirt, folds it, places it on the floor. Her hands are shaking uncontrollably as she struggles with the buttons on her blouse.

The nurse notices the trouble Madeleine is having with her bra. She comes hurrying over, grabs Madeleine by the shoulder, turns her round and unhooks the bra.

'This the first time you've been in a psychiatric hospital, Madeleine?'

'Yes.'

'Don't worry, you'll get used to it.'

The nurse stands there watching, arms crossed, feet apart, eyes boring into flesh as Madeleine steps into the bath.

'Why are you staring at me?'

'We've got to be sure you don't do anything silly.'

'With a cake of soap?'

Madeleine washes herself quickly. She pulls out the plug. The machine is whirring so fast it makes her feel dizzy. The darting pains are also more intense. She leans forward, places a hand on the edge of the bath, ready to support herself, as she steps over the edge, one foot at a time.

'Can I have a towel, please?'

'I have to examine you first.'

'Examine me?'

'Don't worry, it's just routine. I have to be sure you haven't tucked something away in your private parts.'

'What?'

The nurse tells Madeleine to lean over, place both hands on the side of the bath and then spread her legs. The agitation in her belly pauses, then settles into a dull ache. The machine has closed down. Madeleine does as she is told.

The nurse selects a key from the bunch on her waistband and inserts it into the lock on the cupboard door. From the top shelf she takes a pair of rubber gloves and a small torch.

Donning the gloves, she switches on the torch, crouches low, waving the torch along the crack of Madeleine's backside, paying particular attention to the anus. Next, she instructs Madeleine to turn round sideways and place one foot on the edge of the bath.

'That's it. Now bend your knees a little.'

Again Madeleine does as she is told. The nurse shines the light upwards, using her fingers to probe Madeleine's pubic area. Madeleine recalls something her mother once told her about internal examinations. 'Doctors aren't interested in you,' her mother had insisted, staring at her daughter fiercely, as though Madeleine had been accusing the local doctor of assault, '. . . As far as doctors are concerned, you're just a slab of meat.'

Satisfied finally, the nurse stands up and walks over to the cupboard. She fiddles with the torch before placing it back on the top shelf. She peels off the gloves, holds them away from her body, and passes Madeleine a towel with her free hand. Handling the gloves with care, the nurse squeezes them into a flat cellophane packet, seals the opening by pressing it tight, then slips the packet into her uniform pocket.

From a lower shelf she takes a folded square of white cotton cloth. Holding it firmly, she shakes it free of its folds. The words 'Parramatta Hospital' can clearly be read in a circle of faded red ink in one corner of the front edge. It is exactly the same type of hospital gown Madeleine has worn on two separate occasions in the labour ward at Crown Street Women's Hospital.

The tie-strings, sewn several inches apart either side of the open back, are quite important. If the strings are left dangling the nightgown will fall off. Madeleine slips her arms through the sleeves, and the nurse ties two loose bows. Madeleine makes a move towards her pile of clothes.

'I've already told you, Madeleine, you won't be needing your things while you're in this ward.'

'My pants? Can't I wear my pants?'

'The ward is quite warm, you won't need them.'

'I don't want to walk around like this.'

She holds her downturned palms open, indicating the length of the nightgown. It is well above her knees. The nurse makes no reply. The matter is closed. Madeleine tries to remember if the other women are wearing hospital gowns. Surely she would have noticed if they'd been as short as this?

She waits while the nurse locks the cupboard, clips the keys back in place on her belt, spreads the damp towel over the edge of the bath, then heads for the door. Madeleine follows, grateful that the nurse hasn't turned round to see her swoop down and snatch up her pants. There is only one place she can think of to hide them.

Holding the bottom edge of the gown tightly against the backs of her legs, Madeleine follows the nurse into the ward, her pants nestled in her armpit, underneath the gown.

The woman opposite is painting. She sits sideways, legs dangling, bedclothes modestly tucked around her, wielding an inch-wide brush. The brush doesn't look right. It's more suitable for painting a window than a work of art.

The square board is across the woman's knees, held upright in her left hand. Scattered around are several opened tubes of paint, oozing bright colour onto thickly folded sheets of newspaper. Each swipe of the brush adds another daub of brilliance.

Madeleine is mesmerised, caught up with what the woman is trying to express. She knows about those ever-widening circles of colour, that heaving whirlpool pulling her towards something so powerful it could suck her into its depths without warning, no matter how much she struggles.

Paint has dribbled through some of the circles. Madeleine is sure these are meant to indicate tears mixed in with blood and guts.

Suddenly the woman springs to her feet. Bedclothes, tubes of paint and jumbled-up sections of newspaper follow in her wake. Holding the canvas above her head, she races down the ward then back again, whooping and yelling, apparently unconcerned that her nightgown is up around her waist. The nurse with the keys comes running, but before she can get close the woman has turned the canvas on its side and sent it across the floor.

Now she is laughing uncontrollably, arms wrapped around her upper body, head thrown back. Each burst of sound lingers in the air like a sob. Choosing her moment carefully, the nurse grabs the woman's arm, bending it at the elbow in one swift movement, pushing it upwards behind the woman's back, forcing her to drop face-down between two beds.

'Nurse Dumbrell, Jean's acting up again. Will you get a hypodermic ready please, and hurry.'

The woman on the floor is defiant, thrashing about and yelling curses. The nurse holds on tight, shoving her knee into the small of the woman's back. The grim set of her mouth sends a tremor of panic through Madeleine. She wishes the woman would stop resisting. Doesn't she understand how futile her protest is?

Seconds later, another nurse joins the fray. She clutches a stainless-steel kidney bowl, which clatters when she sets it down on the bedside cupboard. She sorts through various items, then holds aloft a syringe, inserts the needle end into an upturned vial and draws back the plunger, sucking the contents into the syringe. Returning the vial to the kidney bowl, she depresses the plunger slightly. A tiny mist of spray shoots into the air.

The woman knows what's coming. She lets forth a stream of abuse and struggles even more. The nurse with the keys yanks hard on the woman's arm.

'Jean, we can do this the easy way or the hard way, it's up to you. What's it to be?'

'Fascist, Nazi, bitch, whore, slut, you fuckin' cow, owwwwwh . . .'

A glint of steel is all Madeleine sees as the point of the needle sinks deep into the woman's thigh. There is silence in the ward for the mere flicker of a second, and then the day gets going again.

The woman's body is limp now, slumped in a heap on the floor. Releasing her grip, the nurse leans forward to turn the woman's head to one side. Almost immediately the loud, snortled breathing changes to a dull snore. A blanket is thrown over the woman and she lies there like a child, like a child that has run and skipped and danced until exhaustion takes over and she drops in her tracks, unable to skip another beat.

Madeleine keeps looking at the clock. She waits fifteen minutes, another ten, then slowly, calmly, as though it is no big deal, she walks a few steps past the end of her bed to retrieve the painting. She is relieved to see it is face up, and the wet paint hasn't smudged.

There is a narrow windowsill behind Madeleine's bed, wide enough to serve as a shelf; she puts the painting there. Throughout the afternoon and early evening she invents excuses to get out of bed. She goes to the toilet, fluffs up her pillows, straightens the coverlet, tucking in the corners for the umpteenth time. When she's sure no one is looking she devours the painting with her eyes. Those bold, vivid strokes satisfy something within her, as though a connection has been made or a straight line drawn between the chaos she feels inside and the whorls of colour in the painting.

Madeleine feels oddly responsible for the woman on the floor. If only she could reassure her that everything will be all right. The very least she can do is safeguard the painting. She will hand it back when the woman wakes up. Madeleine is certain the artist hadn't intended to destroy her work; she just didn't know what to do with all that pain.

In the gaps between worrying about the artist and admiring her work, Madeleine counts. There are three hundred and sixty-seven circles in the cotton coverlet on her bed, an unlikely number for an oblong piece of material. Why not three hundred and seventy or four hundred? This is a mystery that needs further investigation.

It isn't easy to count. Madeleine keeps losing her place. She longs to touch each row of circles, but that would be too easy. Besides, it would give the game away—everyone would know she was mad for sure. The temptation makes her fingers twitch, but she is strong. She won't give in. She has to count several sections twice because the totals won't stay put; they jump around in her brain. It would be so much easier if she could simply tot up the numbers on a piece of paper. She tries to count and rhyme at the same time.

Two, four six, eight,
poor Jean is in a sorry state,
ten, twelve and then fourteen,
up and over, in between,

sixteen, eighteen and along comes twenty,
that's piddle in the middle of a . . . what rhymes
with twenty? Plenty? Mintie? Yes. Mintie will do.
It's moments like these you need Minties or . . .
a calculator, or pen and paper, a distracting caper.

Madeleine laughs at her own silliness.

Down near the locked door a nurse is writing up her notes. She looks up when she hears a soft chuckle. Madeleine appears to be laughing at something. She is standing beside her bed, one hand clapped over her mouth, staring at Jean's artwork.

Sensing she is being watched, Madeleine spins on her heel, making eye contact with the nurse. Both women avert their eyes. Madeleine is already putting the nurse out of her mind. She traces a circle, feeling the raised-up material as a blind person might, exploring the texture, rubbing it between her fingers as though some message might be passed from the coverlet via her fingertips.

Madeleine doesn't see the nurse sort through the files on her desk, alight on Madeleine's name, open the appropriate file and write something down.

The night staff are working in pairs, both sides of the ward, straightening bed covers, pouring water into plastic cups, handing out medication. Jean, the woman on the floor, begins to groan. She tries to sit up, but is so groggy she has to lie down again. Two nurses help her into bed. Madeleine can tell that Jean is only dimly aware of her surroundings.

Soon it is lights-out time. The room is quiet. Madeleine lies in the dark listening, waiting for some sign that will let her know Jean is awake. Minutes later she hears muffled crying. She slips out of bed and creeps across the ward.

'Is there something you need? Should I call the nurse?'

'Don't you bloody dare.'

'I won't if you don't want me to . . .'

'I just said, didn't I?'

'I love your painting. I've got it at the back of my bed. Do you want me to get it for you?'

'No, but if you love it so much you can buy it.'

'Really? How much?'

'How much you got?'

'About $25.'

'That'll do.'

'I'll ask the nurses to get it for you tomorrow.'

Despite the cold, Madeleine stands there waiting. She wants to ask if Jean is feeling OK. She waits a few minutes more, then leans over and looks closely at the face on the pillow. Jean's eyes are closed.

Back in bed, Madeleine can't believe her luck. The painting is hers. John will probably be annoyed about the money, but she doesn't care. Beneath her delight something is bothering her. What is it? She sees again the painting spinning across the floor, the nurse astride Jean's back. That knock-out injection is used like some kind of punishment. Would that happen to her? Surely not. Well, not if she behaves herself. Maybe the nurses would have been kinder if Jean hadn't acted so . . . so wild? Yes, it was Jean's fault; the nurses had no choice. After all, what are they supposed to do? Stand by and let patients run riot?

Madeleine sleeps better that night, better than she has for weeks. Had anyone asked her, she would have said it was because of the painting.

I remember blue finger paint and swirly lines on paper. It was my first day at school. The headmistress was annoyed. 'This child should have been here a year ago,' she said through tight lips. My mother hit back. 'She's been a big help at home, particularly since the new baby came along. Besides, does a year matter that much?'

I watched Miss Gately's face. Would she let me stay? I could count to thirty and I knew my colours. Tim had taught me about the alphabet too, but I always got stuck after ellemenopee. Just then Miss Gately smiled. I heard my mother's chair scrape backwards as she got up to leave. Miss Gately took my hand and we stood there together waving goodbye. A moment later, down a long corridor, we turned left into a classroom with tall windows that overlooked the playground.

The children all had coloured fingers. I watched, fascinated, as they dipped into pots of brightly coloured paint. The teacher led me to a table where there was space for one more. Eager to get started, I reached over to grasp a pot of paint. Ten fingers of blue wriggled up and down the sheet of white paper. Snail fingers. Caterpillar fingers. Blue ribbon trails. I marvelled at the silky feel of paint on my cheek. There were no empty spaces on my page. There were no empty spaces in my head.

This morning Madeleine has an appointment with Dr Beckman, the psychiatrist in charge of Ward 60. Nurse Dumbrell passes on this information as they walk along the windy road through the hospital grounds. Madeleine has been allowed to wear her own slippers and dressing gown. The hem of the dressing gown brushes against her bare legs. It's cold out in the open.

Thin fingers of light creep along the path, nervous fingers that flicker and flutter, distracted by the wind that whistles through the trees. The brick buildings have moss growing up the walls, dense blackness obscuring each doorway. The air is unpleasantly damp, like a funeral on a wet day. Many of the trees have gnarled aerial roots that look like arthritic limbs. Menacingly they creep across the grass, taking up more and more space. These trees are the stuff of nightmares or fairy tales about goblins eager to gobble up unsuspecting children. Madeleine and Nurse Dumbrell pass a fountain, one of many dotted around the grounds. The design is two circular layers on a long thick stem, the smaller layer on top. Weeds thrive in the dirt that has collected over many years. Madeleine sees a young girl, a ballerina wearing her tutu. She has long since been abandoned, imprisoned in stone, waiting. For what? So many ballerinas, waiting, waiting.

Nurse Dumbrell quickens her pace. Madeleine is anxious the nurse will break into a run at any moment. Wait, Mummy, wait.

They enter a building close to the entrance gates. Nurse Dumbrell knocks on the first door down a narrow corridor.

'Come in,' a man's voice calls.

The nurse opens the door and pushes Madeleine forward into the room.

'I've brought Madeleine over to see you, Doctor.'

'Thanks, Nurse. You'll wait outside, will you?'

'If it's all right with you, Doctor, I'll come back and collect her later. We're one nurse short today . . .'

'Fine.' He looks at his watch. 'Say half an hour?'

Madeleine hears the door closing behind her. She feels rooted to the floor.

The doctor sits at a desk. He is writing. The desk is a long way away. Madeleine can see shelves and books but little else. This is not what she expected. She thought he'd have a couch, one of those long sofa thingies with a curved arm at one end, made of plush red velvet or maybe dark brown leather. She'd be asked to lie down. He would sit to one side, asking questions, taking notes. An hour would pass in this fashion. She would be in a dreamy state, untroubled by his gentle probing, relishing the attention, longing to learn from the insights he would offer, passed over one by one, like a collection of shells gathered from a faraway beach only he knew how to find. He'd help her understand what was wrong. Isn't that what psychiatrists do? Isn't that why she agreed to come into hospital? Is this man the type to collect shells?

Madeleine edges further into the room. She is unwilling to look at the doctor. Disappointment tastes bad in her mouth, sticks all the way down her throat. She cannot find the word. It is something that happens in her body; it does not exist as a thought in her mind.

The machine is hissing madly. Can he hear it? She wants to run away. Wait, Mummy, wait. Concentrate, concentrate. There's nothing to be afraid of, he's a doctor, he knows about minds.

Madeleine stares at the window behind the doctor's desk. Curtains stretch from floor to ceiling. Why are they closed? Chinks of light between the lengths of curtain form vertical stripes on the floor and across one end of the desk. She waits for the doctor to speak.

There are two chairs in the room. Dr Beckman is sitting on the bigger one. Now he is leaning forward slightly, elbows resting on the shiny polished desk, fingertips strumming a silent rhythm against his lips.

Madeleine sits down hesitantly on the vacant chair, wondering if she should have asked permission first. The doctor sighs. His fingers fly about in front of his chest. Then, as though making up his mind about something, he looks at her and smiles.

The pump inside Madeleine is thumping away like a big bass drum. She can hear the familiar swish-swish and imagines floodgates opening somewhere close by. What is the doctor saying? She struggles to hear him.

'Madeleine, I'm going to ask you a few questions. You must answer as clearly as you can. Do you understand?'

She nods her head. *Please, just get on with it.*

'Who is the Prime Minister of Australia?'

Does he think I'm an idiot?

'Harold Holt.'

'Now, what does it mean if I say a rolling stone gathers no moss?'

What did he say?

The clock on the desk is ticking loudly. The sound adds volume to the noise of the pump and the raging swirl of water. Madeleine wants to get up and run. This very instant. She grips the sides of the chair with both hands, willing herself to remain in her seat.

The noises vanish. The swishing recedes, leaving an echo in her ears. Madeleine shakes her head back and forth. Is this the pause before a greater onslaught? She stares at the floor and watches an unearthly silence creep into the room. It curls around her chair, wispy and white, then rises, a thick band of smoke, stretching between her and the doctor, absorbing all the air in the room. She has to speak. Something bad will happen if she doesn't.

'Um, um, I suppose, does it mean that the stone is tumbling along so fast it . . . it can't find a resting place?'

'And how would you explain "people who live in glasshouses shouldn't throw stones"?'

Madeleine's mind is a blank. Did she answer him or not? He's writing something down, so perhaps she did. The clock ticks in the background. There is no other sound.

The silence dips and slides along the floor. Madeleine turns her head in time to see it disappear underneath the door. The doctor is still writing. Faces leer at Madeleine from above his head. Can they read what he has written?

The doctor has finished.

'You can wait outside, Madeleine. A nurse will be along to fetch you quite soon.'

She stands in the draughty corridor, shivering. It seems a long time before anyone comes.

IN-PATIENT HISTORY AND PROGRESS NOTES

V.C.N. Blight, Government Printer

SURNAME	FIRST NAMES	AGE	SEX	WARD
ROBERTS	MADELEINE		F	60

DATE	HISTORY AND PROGRESS NOTES

Voluntary admission.

Referred via Out-Patients's Dept.
Original referral from patient's GP,
Dr L Gardiner, Cabramatta.

Proverbs   "Rolling stone ..." Correct interpretation,
rather literal, pushing for further elaboration,
said stone tumbling so fast it can't find a
resting place.

"Glasshouses ..."
Some hesitation in reply – finally said it's rather
obvious some people live in glass houses and
some people throw stones.

Sufficient evidence for diagnosis of schizophrenia.

1. Thought disordered – no organic causes
Disoriented, Inosymatic proverb response
Despite apparent verbal facility quite lost for
words on subjective feelings.

2. Thought content. Almost a closed system

3. Presentation very suggestive of delusions

4. Hallucinations? Hearing own thoughts &c

Depersonalisation – feels like another mind is present.
Suggestive schiz feature.

Diagnosis: Schizophrenia.

The ward is busy. Breakfast dishes are being cleared away, Nurse Dumbrell is handing out medicines from the trolley, and two junior nurses are stripping one of the beds nearest to the locked door. Edna, the woman who used to occupy that bed, has been up for hours. She's wearing her own clothes and has been given permission to dab on rouge and lipstick for this special occasion. Edna's suitcase is on the floor beside her chair. She strokes the handle absent-mindedly and smiles at the nurses as they move back and forth.

Madeleine props herself against the pillows, wiggling her shoulders. She woke this morning with a stiff neck. Now the stiffness is creeping down her back. Edna catches Madeleine's eye.

'My big day.'

Madeleine manages a wobbly smile in reply.

Nurse Dumbrell pauses with the medicine trolley and leans over to pat Edna's shoulder.

'Now, don't get your hopes up too high, Edna. What did Doctor say? One step at a time.'

Edna nods her head.

'I know, Nurse, I know.'

Nurse Dumbrell continues as though Edna hasn't spoken.

'You'll like it in the open ward, you can come and go a bit, walk round the grounds . . .'

Jean is at the end of her bed, hands on hips. She looks down her nose at Nurse Dumbrell.

'How do you know she'll like it? She's still locked up, ain't she? She's still in this bloody loony bin, so don't make out like it's some ritzy hotel.'

'Now, Jean . . .' Nurse Dumbrell warns.

'Now, Jean.' Jean repeats the words and with a few

mincing steps comes closer to the trolley. Nurse Dumbrell wags a finger.

'Get back into your bed, or . . .'

'Or what?'

Jean gives the trolley a shove, but Nurse Dumbrell is too quick. She halts the trolley's momentum, pulling it out of Jean's reach.

Jean dances a little jig on the spot.

'Almost had you that time, Dumb-bell.'

She sniggers and walks back to her bed.

Minutes later one of the junior nurses escorts Edna out of the ward. Madeleine raises her arm to wave. A shooting pain travels up from her fingers.

The stiffness in Madeleine's neck and back is worsening. She pulls back the covers and slowly, carefully, one leg at a time, shifts herself into a sitting position on the edge of the bed. Maybe if she walks around for a while the stiffness will go away. The moment her feet touch the floor, sharp pains course along her spine. Thrown off-balance, she falls across the bed, landing heavily on her left side, her body contorting into an unnatural arch. She is caught in a vice-like grip, stomach protruding, head pushed back to an extreme angle. The pain is excruciating. The machine? Is this the next stage of its takeover?

Breathless with shock, Madeleine attempts to move onto her back. Her legs won't budge. She points the toes of one foot and then the other. The right leg seems OK, but her left foot is going numb. Concentrating so hard perspiration breaks out on her forehead, she wills her right knee to bend until she can feel her toes grip the edge of the bed. If she can just drag herself forward she might be able to bring her left leg into a more comfortable position. She sinks her teeth into her bottom lip to stop herself from screaming.

Using her elbow as a lever and pushing down on her right leg, Madeleine heaves her body further onto the bed. The pain eases slightly, but the numbness in her left foot is moving up towards her ankle.

She wiggles the fingers of her left hand and waves her right arm about. No restriction of movement there. She pats herself down as best she can, then remembers her nightgown. She tugs at the hem. Thank God she still has her knickers on. The only time she takes them off now is for a shower. So far she's been able to dampen the crutch with soapy water each morning, but she hates having to wear the same pair all the time. Still, rough modesty's better than bare-bum cleanliness any day. Good God, here she is, writhing in agony, about to lose her body to a machine, and all she can think about is her knickers? She *must* be mad.

From somewhere behind her head Madeleine hears a voice.

'What's wrong with you, Madeleine?'

Can't she see?

'It's my back. Please, Nurse, could you help me sit up?'

'Can you move your fingers?'

'Yes.'

Madeleine demonstrates by clenching and unclenching her fists.

'And your arms?'

This time Madeleine demonstrates with her right arm, bending it at the elbow then straightening it out.

'I can't tell for sure about the left one, but I think it's OK.'

'What about your legs?'

Madeleine lifts her right leg slightly and winces with pain.

'I don't think I can move it more than that. My left leg is the worst – I can hardly tell if it's still there.'

'I'm going to lift you towards the pillows. When I say "three" try to come with me. One. Two. Three.'

The nurse grunts. Madeleine shifts slightly and cries out. She feels herself falling, falling. She thinks she can hear a plane roar overhead, then she is plunged into a strange, eerie silence.

Nurse Dumbrell's voice is coming from a long way off.

'I think you might be having a reaction to your medication, Madeleine. I'm going to leave you now to phone Dr Beckman. He'll probably prescribe an injection. That'll take care of this problem. Can you hear me?'

Speechless with panic, Madeleine is unable to reply. Saliva dribbles out of her mouth. The tightness in her throat makes each effort to swallow more and more difficult. She thinks she can see John looking at her, but he's upside down and floating in water. She wants to call out. Her lips move but the words won't come.

She hears someone screaming. Is Jean in trouble again?

'Screaming won't help, Madeleine. We're doing our best. Dr Beckman isn't in the hospital right now. I've sent for another doctor. Just stay calm – panicking won't solve anything.'

Much later Madeleine hears a man's voice close to her ear.

'I'm going to give you an injection, Madeleine. It will work immediately but first I have to make sure you're fully conscious. Do you know what day it is?'

What day is it?

How many days has she been here? Five? Six? She can't remember.

'What's your husband's name?'

'Jooooooohn.'

'What was your maiden name?

This time she can't answer at all, but she manages to blink and move her head slightly.

'All right, Nurse, let's move her onto her stomach.'

Madeleine feels a wrenching pain in her neck. It is so severe she thinks she'll pass out. A sharp jab in her backside brings her round. Someone is rubbing the area vigorously. She must have fainted. When she opens her eyes again she is sitting up in bed.

'We've given you a muscle relaxant, Madeleine. You'll be all right in a minute. Do you need to be sick?'

As if on cue her stomach heaves, the tightness in her throat loosens. Vomit spurts out of her mouth, spattering the doctor's clothing. A trapdoor opens and she drops into a foggy abyss, but not before she registers the stern disapproval on the doctor's face.

....

Nurse Dunne is on night duty. She has Madeleine's file open on the desk and is flipping through it, reading various comments made since Madeleine's admission on 23 August.

Aug 23: 1 p.m.   Pt admitted in a depressed state. Looks older
                   than 28 years. Appears anxious and
                   withdrawn.

                                          A. Dumbrell

Aug 23: 11 p.m.   Pt refused to remove underwear, complained
about hospital nightgown being 'too short'.

                                                A. Dumbrell

Aug 24: 4 p.m.   Pt has been weeping on and off all afternoon,
seems distracted and could be hallucinating.
Appearance has deteriorated.
Suspect she has not combed her hair today.

                                                A. Dumbrell

Aug 26: 4 a.m.   Pt awoke from nightmare at 3 a.m. Could not
be calmed.
Largactil 25 mg (to thigh) at 3.30 a.m.

                                                A. Dumbrell

Nurse Dunne turns a few more pages and reads the last
entry.

Aug 27: 4 p.m.   Hd's first visit not a success. Nurse Dumbrell
explained in my hearing that Dr would not
allow a family visit before today but pt was not
satisfied. Seems to think it's hd's fault. Pt asked
him to leave 20 mins after he arrived. Pt quite
distressed after he'd gone. Largactil 25 mg
(to thigh) 3.30 p.m.

                                                J. Dunne

Nurse Dunne begins to write.

Sept 2: 11 p.m.   Pt upset since early evening, has developed
attachment to another pt's artwork, says it
speaks to her. Largactil 25 mg (to thigh)
approx. 8.50 p.m.

                                                J. Dunne

Dr Beckman has a file open on his desk. He interrupts his reading from time to time and glances across at Madeleine. She's too busy to notice, her attention caught on this occasion by the faded appearance of the carpet. Madeleine doesn't like the geometric design, but can't stop herself from counting the interlocking squares and triangles. Dr Beckman notices that her lips are moving. He makes a note on her file.

His words break the silence. Madeleine jumps, but she does not look at him.

'Tell me about your sons, Madeleine. I see here you've got two. What are their names?'

Madeleine drags her eyes away from the carpet. Was it the fourth square across or the fifth?

'I'm sorry, what did you say?'

'I asked about your children. What are their names?'

'Michael and Christopher.'

Madeleine is filled with longing. When will she see them again?

'Michael's nearly three, Chris was eight months old last week, he's been quite ill, he . . .'

'Who's looking after them?'

'. . . had an operation.'

'Did you hear me, Madeleine? I asked who's looking after them?'

'My mother-in-law mostly, but Lindy is only two doors up the street, she's helping out too. She's got three of her . . .'

'I see in this letter your local doctor treated you for back pain earlier this year.'

'Yes, I was in traction for a month. They said . . .'

'Do you hear voices, Madeleine?'

No, not voices, ask me about machines.

Dr Beckman softens his voice to a conspiratorial whisper. 'The nurses tell me you seem distracted a lot of the time. People are often like that when they are hallucinating. Do you know what I'm talking about, Madeleine?'

Hallucinating?

She stares at the carpet. How many feet have tapped out a code on this very spot? Even now the soles of her slippers might be sending out a signal.

Squares and triangles bounce yo-yo fashion in front of her eyes. Triangles and squares, triangles and squares, how ridiculous they look – little flying saucers, whizzing across the carpet with a message from outer space. Hmm. If she divides the room in half, using the chair as a central point, she could count her way across the room, two rows at a time, first the squares, then the triangles. The message might depend on knowing exactly how many saucers are hovering in the room.

'If you won't talk to me, Madeleine, I can't help you.'

Thirty-two, thirty-four, thirty-six – look at that one in the corner, trying to hide under the skirting board. Did you think I wouldn't see you? Thirty-eight, forty, forty-two . . .

. . . .

Madeleine bursts into the crowded waiting room. Her six-week-old son, Christopher, is in her arms. The older boy, Michael, trots alongside, struggling to keep up. The baby's eyes are shut, and his face is tear-stained. Madeleine tries in vain to soothe him.

'Christopher is very ill, Mrs Williams. I think it's serious. Would you mind asking Dr Gardiner if he'll see me right away?'

The receptionist is in no mood to be persuaded. Patients have to wait their turn.

'All these other people are waiting too, you know. What if any of them were to ask for special treatment?'

Madeleine refuses to sit down. The baby's cries become more insistent. She holds him away from her and notes the red, contorted face. There's a towel draped over her shoulder. She adjusts it hastily and positions Christopher upright against her chest, making sure his mouth is close to a section of towel.

As usual, she has misjudged his aim. The long, yellow stream of vomit hits the air like water from a hose, creating a widening pool on the carpet. Michael pats his mother's leg.

'Our baby's been sick again, hasn't he, Mummy?'

'Yes, love.'

Madeleine wipes Christopher's mouth with a corner of the towel. He coughs and gasps for breath and throws his arms about. She has to hold on firmly to prevent him from squirming out of her grasp.

Turning back to speak to the receptionist, she is temporarily silenced by the hostile face glaring back at her.

The baby's cries start up again.

'I told you he was ill, didn't I?'

The smell of vomit is strong. Madeleine rocks back and forth, murmurs, 'There, there,' over and over again in the baby's ear. She is determined to stand her ground.

Dr Gardiner opens his surgery door. He walks past Madeleine and nods to an elderly patient, signalling that it is his turn.

Dr Gardiner steps around the mess on the floor, intending to ignore what's going on, but Madeleine blocks his path.

'Please, Dr Gardiner, I need to see a specialist. Would you mind giving me a referral? Chris is very ill, and I'm really worried.'

The doctor's glance embraces the row of waiting patients. He sighs and gazes at the ceiling, displaying his frustration.

'I told you last week, Madeleine, Christopher has gastro-enteritis. If you continue with the medicine I prescribed . . .'

'It's more than that, I know it is. I'm asking you politely, Doctor – no, in fact, I'm insisting you give me a referral.'

Christopher's scream pierces the air. He draws breath and screams again. Dr Gardiner takes a pen from the pocket of his white coat and reaches into a stationery cupboard for a pad. Madeleine can see the surgery letterhead printed across the top.

She watches the doctor write a name, an address and a few scrawly sentences, then sign his name at the bottom. He tears off the page, folds it in half and places it in an envelope. Madeleine reaches forward to take it, but the doctor tosses the envelope carelessly onto the floor.

There is a long silence. Dr Gardiner wipes the nib of his pen with a tissue. He pretends he isn't interested in what Madeleine does.

She places a hand on Michael's shoulder.

'See that envelope, Michael? I want you to pick it up for me, there's a good boy.'

The child grasps the envelope between his chubby fingers and passes it to his mother.

Madeleine walks to the door, pulls it open and props her foot against the bottom corner. Michael runs ahead of her.

'Where are we going now?' he asks.

Dr Gardiner is still standing near the desk. Madeleine turns round to shout at him.

'Call yourself a doctor!' she yells. 'You've got the manners of an alley cat!'

She doesn't wait for a reply. She is already on the footpath, juggling Christopher and tearing the envelope open, reading the name of the paediatrician. The address is Murray Street, Liverpool. That's only ten minutes away in the car. She won't bother phoning for an appointment. She'll drive there straight away.

Back in the ward, Madeleine hastens down the corridor of beds and into the toilet. She doesn't want to think, doesn't want to dwell on how she came to be a patient in this bloody place. Fragments of conversation wheel like a flock of magpies above her head, menacing, darting, swooping down, attacking her with sharp beaks.

'Your little boy is very sick, Mrs Roberts. I'm going to have to operate today . . .'

'Piloris stenosis. Roughly translated, it means a tumour in the stomach . . . it affects boys more than girls.'

'No, we can't discharge your baby. He's picked up an infection, and we'll have to keep him in for at least another week, maybe two . . .'

'You were right to get your husband to see me, Mrs Roberts. He does have diabetes, diabetes mellitus. It's a late-onset case, so he'll have to be admitted. We have to get his blood-sugar level right . . .'

'I think we've found the cause of your back pain, Mrs

Roberts. The X-rays show a slipped disc . . . Traction is the best thing . . . You'll probably be in hospital a month or so . . .'

'You've been under a lot of stress, Mrs Roberts. I think a psychiatrist could help . . .'

'Of course you're not mad. It's your nerves – you're probably highly strung. I'd like you to see this specialist I know. He's a good man, one of the best.'

No. No. Leave me alone, go away, go away.

The tiles are cold to the touch. They form horizontal rows from the skirting-board up. There are ninety-seven tiles on the bottom row, ninety-seven and a half on the next. How many rows are there altogether?

A short time later Madeleine is dragged back to her bed by two nurses. She resists their efforts and continues to count.

Dr Alan Gardiner
Albion Street,
Cabramatta

Dear Alan,

<u>Re Madeleine Roberts</u>

Thank you for referring Mrs Madeleine Roberts for psychiatric assessment and treatment. I realise that some of what follows may already be recorded on your file for this patient.

She suffers from Neurotic Depressive Reaction, more marked since the birth of her second child last September. It is quite apparent that she has suffered from character neurosis for many years, but this was brought to a clinical head by the birth of first one child then another and may also connect with some disappointment about the sex of the children. In her case, this neurosis involves dependency conflicts of considerable degree connected to her own childhood.

Owing to an extremely disturbed family history she has previously avoided emotional dependence upon anyone until the time of her marriage. Her husband, from my interview with him last week, would appear to have taken her at face value and assumed that she was the extremely independent person she appeared to be. Instead, she would fundamentally prefer to depend upon him in emotional and practical ways, of which he is allegedly quite unaware.

She had no significantly close friends before marriage, and obviously went into this relationship with a lot of anxiety, and hoping too that she would find something to fill her unanswered childhood needs.

Her family relationships were extremely disturbed. She and her younger brother were the product of her mother's third marriage to a fairly rough type. Six children were born to the mother previously. One of the six died before patient was born. Two of the older children were reared with patient and her brother.

She has no close relationship with her mother. Father administered frequent beatings and other physical cruelty. Patient endeavoured to get between her parents when they were fighting in an attempt to protect Mother. Patient spent her childhood in an atmosphere of disapproval and criticism, exemplified by the Father's statement that she 'would have a kid in her arms by the time she was 16'. Patient tells me she has not seen any of her family for a long time.

Despite this insecure and troubled background, she has worked and cared for herself since leaving school (and home) at 15 and would appear to have a good record of employment. She worked in an office at Parramatta after she was married and left the job six weeks before her first son was born. In spite of her fairly severe and long-standing neurotic problems, she has considerable assets for psychotherapy and would clearly benefit from a fairly long period in analytic psychotherapy, and I feel that at the present stage she has sufficient motivation to go through with this.

Unfortunately, the family income does not stretch to the weekly charge of $6 and patient has also expressed reluctance about leaving the children at night. For this reason I have suggested she be referred to the outpatient department of Parramatta Psychiatric Centre and have provided an assessment letter similar to this one for that purpose.

Many thanks for referring her to me,

Kind regards,

Howard Ferguson

P.S. I saw Bert Fredericks a while back and he asked about you. Maybe we three should make time for a round of golf some time?

John is disturbed by the change in Madeleine. She can hardly keep her eyes open, and when she does look around she appears unable to focus for more than a few seconds. He has to remind her constantly what they've been talking about. What bothers him most is the twitch that has developed on one side of her upper lip. He'd been assured this spell in hospital would do her good. Now he's not so sure.

'Have you been up and about today?'

'Yes, we have a shower at 6.30 . . .'

'Before breakfast?'

He leans over her.

'Madeleine, I asked you a question. Do you have your shower before breakfast?'

'Mmm, as soon as we get up . . .'

She is staring at something over his shoulder. John turns to follow her line of vision. All he can see is a section of the brick wall opposite. Her lips are moving, and she is whispering something. Can she see him? Does she even realise he's here? He sits on the bed and reaches out to stroke a raised lump in the bed that he presumes is her knee. He tries again.

'So what happens after you have a shower?'

'What? What did you say?'

He pats the lump to encourage her.

'You were telling me you have a shower early each morning. What happens after that?'

'Breakfast. No, before that . . .'

Another pat.

'Go on, before that . . .'

'. . . uh, before that . . .'

'What happens before breakfast?'

Madeleine sits up higher in the bed and makes an effort to concentrate. John withdraws his hand.

'The nurses give out cigarettes to those who want them and then . . .'

'Don't tell me you've taken up smoking?'

He's hoping to make her laugh, but she goes on as though he hasn't spoken.

'. . . we have breakfa . . .'

'Does the hospital supply the cigarettes?'

'No, the nurses write the person's name on each packet, but . . .'

'But?'

'I'm sorry, what was I saying?'

He stands up and walks around the end of the bed to the other side.

'You were saying the nurses give out cigarettes before breakfast.'

'Yeah, no one's allowed to have matches or cigarettes in here.'

About to ask why, he stops himself in time. Maybe it's better to keep the questions simple.

'So what do they give you for breakfast?'

'Cereal, cold toast, that kind of thing.'

'Is the food OK?'

'I think so.'

'You think so? Don't you know?'

For the first time Madeleine looks directly at him.

'All I really want to do is sleep. Half the time I don't know what day it is.'

She yawns as though emphasising the point and slides down further in the bed.

John glances up and down the ward in search of a chair.

The woman in the next bed smiles at him. He turns his back on her. Where are visitors supposed to sit? Madeleine's eyes are closed. He looks at her lip. It's as if a fly is trapped under the skin and won't stay still. Does she feel it?

'I hear you're moving into another ward tomorrow. You'll be home before you know it.'

She makes no reply.

Under the covers, she jiggles her feet around and struggles to stay awake. John looks at his watch. Can that be the time? Has he only been here ten minutes?

'The boys are fine. Mum's managing really well, and Lindy's been a great help. I don't think we could cope without her.'

'Do you think she minds?'

'Minds? Why should she? She's your friend, love, she wants to help. By the way, she said to tell you she's coming to visit just as soon as the doctors say it's OK.'

Madeleine narrows her eyes in an attempt to keep his face in focus.

'You mean permission? Who . . . what doctor?'

He speaks slowly to disguise his irritation.

'Dr Beckman. I rang him again the other day. He seems OK – do you think he's all right?'

She sighs wearily.

'I've only seen him twice.'

Her eyelids flutter and close.

John walks back to the other side of the bed.

'I'd better let you get some rest.'

He leans over to kiss her on the cheek.

She doesn't stir.

Nurse Dunne is unlocking the door. She explains that Madeleine is still adjusting to her medication.

'It's only been two weeks. She'll be fine — it's always like this in the beginning.'

Comforted by these words, John walks away.

Madeleine sits in a chair near her bed, dressed and waiting. She holds a painting on her lap, newly signed by the artist. Absent-mindedly her fingers follow the sweeping curve of the signature, tracing the J in Jean, the S in Springer. The machine is quiet. Maybe they've stunned it into submission? If only she didn't feel so tired, so dopey.

A knock on the door attracts the attention of Nurse Dunne. She fits the key into the lock, turns it, pulls the door open. Another nurse waits outside.

'Good morning, Elaine. Is my patient ready?'

'Ready and waiting. Come on, Madeleine, it's time to go.'

It's only a few steps to the open ward. There are no windows, and the cold stone wall behind Madeleine's bed is damp to the touch. Hers is the last bed in the left-hand row of ten. Nurse Kirkby explains the rules while Madeleine packs away her few items of clothing in the chest of drawers alongside her bed.

'We close this ward at nine every morning, so remember to take what you need with you, because you won't be allowed back in till after five o'clock.'

'Where are we meant to go?'

'Anywhere you like. Just don't leave the grounds.'

Nurse Kirkby's laugh is derisive.

'Some women never leave the day-room except to do their washing. Do you know where the laundry is?'

'No.'

'It's on the right through the arch, across from the day-room – you can't miss it. Get your husband to bring you in some pegs. The line's over the back – ask one of the other women to show you. I'm taking your bag, it'll be safe in the storeroom. Have you got everything?'

'I think so.'

'Good. I'll come and collect you from the day-room at lunchtime. You have got a watch, haven't you?'

Madeleine nods.

'Twelve o'clock on the dot. And then' – she pauses to give Madeleine a propelling push towards the door – 'you'll be on your own.'

Lily sits on the floor, legs stretched out in front, back ramrod-straight. She appears unaware of her surroundings, detached, as though her hands and legs belong to someone else. Madeleine has retreated to a nearby corner, wishing she could lie down.

Lily's hands fly across her lap like prancing flamingoes – elegant birds that dip and sway and go off at a tangent. She can't keep this up much longer, can she? Madeleine wants to close her eyes, rest her head on her knees, but she can't. She must keep watch. Someone has to.

Clumsily, the birds knock against each other. Now they are rubbing themselves along the length of those thin, white arms. They make cupping sounds as they connect, palm on palm, then separate, slap, clap, slap.

At last Lily reacts. She pins the flamingoes down, one under each leg, but they writhe and pull against her thighs. Her cheeks are sucked in with the strain. She begins to rock, back and forth, side to side.

Oh, did you see that? They've broken free. One of the flamingoes crashes against her face. The blow catches her at an odd angle. Tears spill out of her eyes. She leans sideways out of reach, but the flamingo strikes again and again and again. How awful. Poor woman. Is that the only way she can speak?

....

Shuffling feet. Body smells. Weary faces. Tables set for four. The scrape of chairs. A door blows open. Someone groans. Close to the counter, it is suffocatingly warm. The queue moves slowly. Three women are serving up plates of food. They are dressed in green uniforms with matching caps.

Tall stacks of heavy, white plates are diminishing rapidly. The first woman grabs a clean plate and doles out mashed potato from the pot in front of her with a wooden spoon. Expertly she crosses one hand over the other and the plate moves along. The next woman is armed with tongs. She snaps up a stringy slice of meat and shakes it firmly. A watery liquid drips back into the metal dish. The woman positions the meat lengthwise, alongside the mashed potato. The third woman is in charge of the gravy. She pours a liberal amount onto each plate. Her face gleams with sweat and her cheeks are flushed deep pink.

On Madeleine's plate, the gravy is sinking through the mashed potato and the meat has almost disappeared beneath the grey, sludgy surface. There's a tray at the end of the counter, piled high with thinly cut slices of white bread. Madeleine is surprised to see patients ahead of her snatching several slices as they pass by. It takes her a moment to work it out, then she too reaches towards the tray. As she walks away from the counter, she can see tubs of margarine on the tables and big jars of jam.

'You can't sit there, that's Judy's place.'

'Go find your own seat! Jenny's been sitting in that chair for as long as anyone can remember.'

Madeleine wanders around the room. At last she finds a table near the door. All four seats are vacant here. She soon learns why. Each time a gust of wind blows the door open, cold air rushes in, alive with tiny bits of grit and dust that swirl and fly in her direction. She feels like crying, but she makes herself chew her jam sandwiches instead.

Madeleine can't find her blouse. She took it off the line yesterday, and distinctly remembers putting it in her bottom drawer. Glancing round, she catches sight of the woman in the next bed. Diane? Yes, that's her name. Diane is looking at her oddly. There's something shifty about that look, as if she's done something wrong.

'You stole my blouse, didn't you?'

'What?'

'It was in my drawer. You took it, didn't you?'

'I don't know what you're talking about. I haven't been anywhere near your bloody drawers.'

'I know you took it. Nurse, Nurse Kirkby, would you please make her give me back my blouse?'

The nurse strides towards the two women.

'What does it look like, Madeleine?'

'It's pink and there's embroidery on the pocket. She asked me yesterday if she could borrow it. I told her she couldn't, so now she's pinched it.'

'Have you looked everywhere?'

'Yes, see for yourself.'

Madeleine keeps her underwear in the top drawer – three pairs of knickers and a bra. When Nurse Kirkby pulls open the next drawer, she sees two pairs of socks, a hairbrush and a small array of toiletries. The last drawer is empty.

'All right, Diane, show me your drawers.'

'Why should I? I haven't got her blouse and I don't want you rifling through my things.'

Nurse Kirkby walks the short distance to the next bed.

'Are you going to open these drawers, Diane, or will I do it for you?'

Diane heads for the door. They can hear her yelling as she moves out of sight.

'You wait, you bloody bitch, I'll get you for this.'

Beneath a pile of magazines in Diane's second drawer Nurse Kirkby finds a pink blouse with embroidery on the pocket. Reaching across the bed, she hands the blouse to Madeleine.

'It's not a good idea to have anything valuable in here, Madeleine. Some of these women are light-fingered, and the staff can't act as watchdogs all the time.'

Madeleine has her arm through one sleeve. She pauses to look at the nurse.

'I don't understand. What am I supposed to do? Carry all my clothes around with me?'

'I can't tell you what to do, I'm simply explaining that we can't be held responsible if things go missing. Now hurry along, it's time you got on with your day. This ward should have been locked ten minutes ago.'

NURSING NOTES WARD 60

Specify Case History or Nursing Notes

V.C.N. Blight, Government Printer

SURNAME	FIRST NAMES	AGE	SEX	WARD
ROBERTS	MADELEINE		F	60

DATE	HISTORY AND PROGRESS NOTES
Sep 14	Pt has needed several days to settle into the routine of the open ward. Reluctant to eat at first, claimed the smell of the food made her ill.
Sep 17	Have noticed involuntary twitching – pt's mouth and both arms. Suggest Dr Beckman be told – he may want to prescribe for side effect symptoms.
Sep 18	Pt's state of mind has deteriorated. Hardly speaks to anyone and has adopted a corner of the day-room as her own. Sits there, not far from the other territorial type – Lily. They do not interact but I have noticed they seem to derive some sort of satisfaction from each other's presence.
Sep 21	Pt refused to acknowledge hd when he visited this morning. Has to be encouraged to get herself to the dining room for meals.
Sep 22	Am concerned about pt's attitude – seems to be retreating further.
Sep 24	Disinterested in moving from day-room.

Every so often odd words like 'baby' or 'jelly' or 'hello' are catapulted into Lily's mouth. She has tried spitting the nasty things out, but they won't budge. Her lips are sore, but she keeps trying.

Someone must have opened her up. She's got proof. There's a scar on her left side – she noticed it a while back. They must have opened her up and stuck all these words inside. They think she doesn't know, but she has her eye on them now. If she's on the floor it won't be so easy to grab her. She'll kick them if she has to.

....

Nurses Kirkby and Padstow agree the best time to get Lily prepared for her transfer to Ward 18 is after the early morning bed-making rush is over.

The patients are returning from the dining hall. Lily sees the nurses. They approach her cautiously. She knows what's going on. Well, they're not going to open her up a second time, that's for sure. They expect her to be hostile, aggressive even, but instead she runs away, down the winding path that everyone knows leads to the river.

Madeleine is wary about drawing attention to herself. She intends to follow Lily, but she doesn't want to be seen. Leaving the path a few yards past the ward, she pushes her way through dense undergrowth. Her pace is unbearably slow and she feels dizzy, but that's probably because of her medication. A low branch scratches her face and arms but she hardly notices. All she can think about is finding Lily before they do, or . . .

....

Nurse Kirkby is very upset. As she explains to Dr Beckman, she and Nurse Padstow went down by the river this morning to look for Lily. When there was no sign of her after almost twenty minutes, Nurse Padstow returned to the ward to alert the others while Nurse Kirkby went on looking.

She was about to give up – it was almost lunchtime, she'd checked the time on her watch – when she heard a woman scream. She doubted it was Lily. After all, the woman had been catatonic for some time. But she hurried along the water's edge in the direction of the scream as fast as she could.

She can't remember how long it took her to reach them, but it must have been a good forty minutes or so. There was no track to speak of, and the sand was soft like quicksand, and she kept tripping over stones and tree-roots. Nurse Kirkby doesn't mention how frightened she was, how often she stopped to take several deep breaths and how she was worried that it might prove foolish to tackle what lay ahead, whatever it was, on her own. In the end she kept going because she couldn't bear the thought of turning back. She has no sense of direction, as her father often tells her.

Lily's clothes were soaking wet, and her face had turned blue. There was no pulse – Nurse Kirkby checked that right away. Madeleine's clothes were damp from the waist down. She must have tried to pull Lily out of the water. Her screams went on and on. No No No No. The one word over and over again. Nurse Kirkby had to slap her face to get her to stop, and she had a dreadful time trying to prise Madeleine's fingers away from the dead woman's shoulders and to get her to leave the body where it lay. She had no intention of moving Lily herself. If anyone asked, she was prepared to say that she hadn't wanted to destroy any evidence.

'Madeleine was still in an hysterical state when I got her back to the ward.'

Again, Nurse Kirkby doesn't mention her own feelings. The sight of the drowned woman's bloated face, the stricken look in Madeleine's eyes, the way her own bowels turned to water.

She pulls a tissue from her uniform pocket and dabs at her eyes.

Dr Beckman strokes his chin and thinks for a moment. It's important that he understands all the details.

'I may have more questions to ask you in the near future, Nurse, but for now I want you to go home and rest. I don't want to see you back here until next week. No, don't worry, I'll inform the Ward Sister myself. You get yourself home to bed. Do you feel up to driving?'

After Nurse Kirkby has gone, Dr Beckman phones through to Ward 60. He gives a few instructions, then asks Nurse Padstow to ring around for a relief nurse.

'Tell them we need someone for at least a week. Got that?'

He puts the phone back on its hook and sits at his desk, doodling on a writing pad, making sucking noises with his mouth. It's an old habit of his, running his top teeth over his bottom lip. He reaches for the phone again, then, with his hand poised over the receiver, he hesitates.

The top sheet of the pad is covered in linked semi-circles. He pulls at the page, tearing it from the pad, screws it into a ball and drops it in the wastepaper bin.

Now he jots down a numbered list.

1. Inform the Superintendent.
   Make an appointment?
   Write a memo?

Walk over unannounced?

Which?

2. Prescribe something for Madeleine.

3. Next of Kin for Lily?

He dials through to Ward 60.

'Nurse Padstow? Dr Beckman here again. The dead woman. What's her surname? OK, I'll hold on.'

Absent-mindedly he draws circles around individual words on his list, then decorates the edge of each circle with a series of wavy lines.

There's something Madeleine's trying to remember, something important. It slips out of her grasp, leaving behind hot, salty tears that stick to her eyelids, obscuring her vision.

The floor seems closer, and Madeleine keeps bumping into doors and chairs and beds. Three times this morning she's bruised her legs against the edge of the coffee table in the day-room.

Nurse Padstow's voice comes from behind.

'No, don't sit down. Keep walking – you need the exercise.'

'But I . . . I feel . . .'

'Doctor's orders. You're getting lazy, Madeleine Roberts. You can't sit around all day – you'll be as fat as a pig rolling in mud if you're not careful.'

Madeleine nods her head obediently and moves towards the door. She has to get away. It's cold outside but the sun is bright, so bright it hurts her eyes. She shambles drunkenly past the entrance to the dining hall and around the corner. She doesn't know where she's heading – anywhere will do, so long as she can sit down.

Minutes later she comes upon a swimming pool. Beyond is a beautifully constructed wall, perfectly smooth, starkly vertical, high enough to create an imposing barrier between the hospital and Parramatta prison. 'Storm the ramparts,' she whispers softly, following one horizontal line of bricks from left to right, tracing the curve to a starting point where brick meets ivy-covered stone, the front boundary wall of the hospital.

She begins to count. How many bricks make a wall? How many bricks make a prison? The opening lines of a poem float into her mind.

Stone walls do not a prison make
nor iron bars a cage . . .

She'd learnt that at school, but what comes next? Already the bright flash of memory is fading, jumping about, defying her efforts to hang on, just like those solid black lines between each row of bricks.

On her hands and knees she counts the third row from the bottom. One hundred and sixty-four, one hundred and sixty-five, one man climbs over the wall, but is he dead or alive? One hundred and sixty-six, one hundred and sixty-seven, what did they do to Lily? And will she go to heaven?

Madeleine comes to an abrupt halt. Lily? Where is Lily? What did they do to her? Something happened, but what?

You'd better watch out,
you'd better not cry,
you'd better be good,
I'm telling you why,
Lily isn't coming to town.

Dr Beckman's elbows are resting on the desk, his alabaster fingers pointing to his chin. Madeleine notices how evenly his nails have been cut, each precise edge a statement about the line that must be drawn between flesh and nail.

He stands up, walks across the room and back again. Long thin fingers, long thin body, shoulders that curve around his chest like a crooked wire coathanger. He leans across the desk, both hands flat on the wooden surface. Spread out like fans, those long, thin fingers take up the space.

'It will help you, Madeleine. Six treatments, that's all. You'll feel groggy for a day or two, but that's because of the anaesthetic.'

She concentrates on taking short, shallow breaths through her nose.

Two hands. Always two. Why not three? Why not one? Does Coathanger Doctor know? His hands say he does. Wouldn't one hand be kinder? Why not one parent?

His fingers are pale, deathly white, cold as ice.

'Ah, there you are! I've got a form here for you to sign.'

Nurse Tasker is waving a carefully folded sheet of paper. She takes a pen from her top pocket and hands it to Madeleine. Keeping a firm grip on one edge, Nurse Tasker rests the folded paper against her bent knee. With her free hand she indicates a line of dots.

'What is this, Nurse?'

'Oh, it's just about your medication. We have to keep records of what each patient is on from one month to another.'

Obediently Madeleine signs her name.

AUTHORIZATION

A123-37 – B   V.C.N. Blight, Government Printer

1.   I accept responsibility for the specific medication administered to me
during my stay in Parramatta Psychiatric Centre.

Signature ....

2.   I give my consent for one (or more) E.C.T. treatments in accordance with
my doctor's instructions.

Signature .... *M. Roberts* ....

3.   I request permission for details of my medical file to be released to:

....

for legal/personal reasons.

Signature ....

The patients scheduled for ECT sit in the day-room, watching the nurses wheel trolley-loads of equipment from the storeroom to the annexe at the far end of the veranda. The nurses chat happily, but none of the patients speak. They sit with hands clenched and stare at the opposite wall.

A nurse gives the signal. The patients line up in the order of seating, the nearest to the door first. There is always a scramble to get that first seat, to get the whole business over and done with as soon as possible. Madeleine has no such enthusiasm; somewhere in the middle will do. She trudges along with the others, tightening her dressing-gown cord into a firmer knot, her gesture an effort to hold herself in check. Shuffling feet provide the only sound as the conga line of misery moves at a funeral-march pace along the veranda.

The first group of six are led through the door. Madeleine is further down the line, but she can see everything. Jenny, a patient from the same ward, is on the bed nearest the door. Her temples are being rubbed with ointment from a big glass jar. Now they are placing sticky-backed metal tabs against her temples. Wires connect the metal tabs to a machine on the bedside cupboard. The machine is a black box with dials and switches on the front. Jenny's right arm is turned so that her palm is facing upwards. The point of a needle sinks into a vein. When it is pulled out the nurse sticks a bandaid over the solitary drop of blood. The doctor nods in Jenny's direction and turns a switch. The nurse presses down on Jenny's chest. Madeleine fixes her attention on the machine. The dial has a black pointer similar to the large hand on a clock. Abruptly the pointer swings to the middle of the dial. It keeps swinging in a small arc. Jenny's body stiffens and twitches. Another five bodies are stiff and twitching. One woman thrashes about, and nurses rush to take up positions both sides of her bed. They hold the woman's body down. It seems a long time before the needle stops swinging. The bodies on the beds make small quivering movements, like fallen leaves hovering above the ground, displaced, unsettled.

Madeleine remembers what the doctor told her yesterday. She mutters his words over and over . . . *this is for your own good, this is for your own good, this is for your own good* . . .

'OK, Madeleine, lie down and give me your arm.'

Madeleine pulls up the sleeve of her dressing gown. The nurse pinches the flesh on the inside of Madeleine's elbow.

'We have a bit of a problem with Madeleine, Doctor. She has elusive veins – we can never find them when we need them.'

'Is that right? And are you elusive too, Madeleine?'

She feels no urge to reply.

After a few attempts the needle goes in. The taste of fried onions fills her mouth.

....

The room spins. Madeleine has a blinding headache. She opens her eyes and closes them again quickly. The light hurts. What's happening?

'Come on, Madeleine, open your eyes, it's all over.'

Over? What's over?

'Come on now, you'll feel better in a moment. Stand up, there's a good girl.'

A nurse walks between Madeleine and another patient, gripping each by the elbow. She steers them along. Madeleine feels dizzy and is grateful when they stop for a moment. She leans against the nurse for support. The other woman stumbles, puts her free hand to her head and moans. They stand there, unable to proceed.

'Just a bit further, Doreen, we're almost there.'

A second nurse takes hold of Madeleine's arm from behind and leads her to a chair.

'We'll bring you a cup of tea in a moment, Madeleine.'

She doesn't realise the nurse is talking to her. *Madeleine? Who's Madeleine?*

......

Days pass in a blur. Monday. Wednesday. Friday. One treatment, two treatments, three. How many times has she sat in the day-room waiting? How many more? Oh dear God, how many more?

The hair around Madeleine's temples is pulled back. Ow, that hurts, don't pull so tight. She must stand still while her hair is plaited. Her mother is always in a hurry. She doesn't see tears well up in Madeleine's eyes. There are no tears now, only a black heaviness followed by exploding lights. See those long streaks of light, there, see them? Criss-crossing searchlights at the Showground in wartime, raking the sky. Ration books, blacked-out windows, barbed wire on Bondi beach, strategies for a time that is starkly different, out of the ordinary.

She'll imagine she's somewhere else. Walking on a beach, feeling sand between her toes, water splashing over her ankles, salty wetness clinging to her legs. Her thoughts are scrambling. She's looking down a telescope, no, it's a kaleidoscope, she can't focus on the moving bits of glass. They slip and slide, dissolve into whirls of colour spinning faster and faster as they are sucked into a gurgling vortex, a large hole in the universe leading to nothingness.

Madeleine blinks. Don't do that, please, don't you know temples are tender? Vulnerable book-ends for the brain. They need careful attention, special treatment in an extra-ordinary time.

That burning smell. Is it her hair? Is it her brain? She mustn't cry, it's for her own good, to make her well again, oh please, just get on with it.

She sees children making animal and bird shadows. The children's hands move back and forth and birds fly across the wall. There's a rabbit. Its ears grow long and pointy like daggers. The rabbit has huge front teeth that gnash noisily and a long, white beard, like – like God. It is coming to get her. Its mouth is open wide. Look at that little girl, hasn't she got fat cheeks, couldn't you eat her all up . . .

Dry mouth. Thick tongue. She tries to speak. Words won't come. Trapped. Flies caught in honey. She has to help them escape. She has to . . . tell him, has to . . . make him understand.

Dr Beckman waits patiently. He can see she is making an effort.

'How . . . many . . . more . . .'

Madeleine runs her tongue over her lips in an attempt to ease the dryness.

'. . . treatments must . . . I have . . . Doctor?'

His words skate across ice, forming fast-moving figures of eight, full of colour and light. So much light, so much colour, he might easily break into song.

'As many as I think necessary, Madeleine, no more, no less.'

'But how . . . how many . . . is that, Doctor?'

Dr Beckman rocks back and forth on his heels. He makes

big gestures with his hands, pushing his arms out from his chest as though ready to embrace the world.

'Don't pin me down, Madeleine. We'll find out soon enough.'

....

I walk past the basketball court on my way to the chapel. Girls are sitting on wooden benches in twos and threes, eating sandwiches, chatting and laughing. I hurry past them. At the arched doorway I dip the fingers of my right hand into the holy-water container fixed to the wall, make the sign of the cross and head for my favourite spot, the third pew from the front. I don't kneel or say a prayer, but sit there staring at the mural that takes up most of the space between the altar and the high-pitched roof.

His head and shoulders rise above a billowing cloud. Blue marble-chip eyes stare at me from beneath eyebrows as thick and white and bushy as his prophet-like beard. One hand reaches through the cloud towards his only son. Strict and aloof, this is a cruel, demanding father, a cruel, demanding god.

Idly I trace the path of several baby-sized angels, chubby and partly clad, ascending to heaven either side of the adult Jesus. His face is in profile, turned upwards, eager for the first glimpse of home, one hand discreetly pointing to his exposed heart. I yearn with him. I want a home too.

If God is so knowing, so all-seeing, then he must know how bad things are in our house. Does he see my mother's black eyes, the beatings we kids get? Does he feel the tension, the panic? Can he see the agony in my exposed heart?

My attention is fixed on three dainty droplets of blood positioned in an orderly vertical row below the heart, like tears falling from a cheek. There is nothing bloody or messy about these majestic red droplets. This is blood that will not stain. Royal blood, unreal, suspended on the wall for ever. A coded message for Catholics. Don't bring your troubles here.

Cleanliness is next to godliness. No mess. No gore. Only God's law.

It's Tuesday morning. Lindy is driving back from the hospital. She feels compelled to act, to do something. She can't wait for John to arrive home from work. Even another hour might be too late. She turns the car around and heads into town, to the garage where John works.

An elderly man points her in the direction of a truck up on blocks in a far corner of the workshop.

The cement floor is greasy with oil stains. Cars and tools fill every inch of available space. Men in blue overalls, surprised to find a woman in their midst, greet her with mocking eyes. Wisecracks form quickly on their tongues, ready to pounce. Lindy doesn't notice. She picks her way around the obstacles, trying not to mind the smell of grease and car fumes.

'Lindy! What the hell are you doing here?'

John is standing under the truck. Hurriedly he drops the spanner and pulls a cloth from his back pocket.

'If you could see the state of her, John – she looks terrible. I know they said we should stay away till the treatments are finished, but I tell you, seeing her there today, it's enough to give anyone nightmares.'

John continues to wipe his hands, slow movements that make Lindy want to scream. She follows him around to the front of the truck, away from prying eyes and straining ears.

'Dr Beckman said . . .'

'John, you should see her yourself – forget what he says. For God's sake, she's been there five months, and she's not getting better, she's getting worse. She carries that dreadful bloody painting under her arm and she can't even sit still. She paces up and down all the time. I couldn't get her to stop or even sit down, and she hardly seems able to recognise her own name. I think we'll lose her entirely if you don't do something.'

Dr Beckman checks through the filing cabinet, removes a file and returns to sit at his desk. He finds the most recent page of notes, hurriedly reads through what he's written and picks up the telephone receiver to resume his conversation.

'Yes, Mr Roberts, your wife is booked in for her twelfth treatment tomorrow.'

He fiddles with the telephone cord, grabbing it and then letting it go.

'What's that? Six? Well, I might have said at least six . . .'

Nodding his head, he adopts a hearty tone of voice.

'Well, I saw her only yesterday and I think she is showing definite signs of improvement.'

There is a pause. He continues to nod his head.

'Of course you're worried, yes, yes, but I did warn you that the accumulated effects of the anaesthetic take a while to wear off.'

He wraps the telephone cord around his fist, pulling it tight.

'I see. Yes, I do understand. No, I don't plan any more treatments after tomorrow, but I'm sure you'll agree how unwise it would be to stop this course of treatments now, when we're so close to the end.'

Slowly he unwinds the cord and swings it back and forth, freeing one or two kinks.

'Yes, we'll see how she is by the end of the week. ECT is not a miracle cure, of course, but it does have a remarkably high success rate.'

Dr Beckman speaks faster. He's ready to wind up the conversation.

'No trouble at all. Any time, Mr Roberts. You did say you're coming to my talk? Oh, good. I look forward to seeing you. Seven o'clock, that's right. There'll be a notice with directions near the front gate. Right then. Goodbye, Mr Roberts, No. NO. I'm very glad you rang, no trouble at all.'

....

Dr Beckman is running late. He walks down the brightly lit hallway of the administration building to the far end. The meeting room isn't very big, but it is large enough to accommodate the forty or so people who are here tonight, seated on five rows of plastic chairs facing a long table. Dr Beckman proceeds down the middle aisle, heading straight for the table to join the Medical Superintendent, Dr Keller, and two other members of staff who have already addressed the audience. Dr Beckman stands to one side while Dr Keller introduces him.

Perching on the edge of the table, he moves one of the water jugs and a clean glass within easy reach. He looks up then and recognises a man in the third row and a grey-haired couple sitting one side of the middle aisle on his left. He apologises for his late arrival and begins his speech with the same opening remark he made to a group of first-year nurses just last week.

'You've probably heard a variety of comments about ECT. Rarely, and I do mean rarely, are such comments accurate. It is more likely that what you've heard is a potent mix of unfounded rumour and misinformation.'

He pours a glass of water from the jug and takes a few slow sips.

'You have entrusted us with the care of your loved ones, and we want you to have confidence in our care and concern for them. Now, can I take that as an accepted starting point for us all?'

He expects to hear softly spoken replies of 'yes', or 'of course', but what he looks for is a frown, a set jaw, some indication of resistance or doubt. He spots such a face in the second row. She's wearing a grey dress. Her eyes hold him at a distance. He moves his glance past her to the man a few seats along who is chewing his bottom lip.

'Thank you. I am encouraged by your understanding. Now, let me begin with the big question. What *exactly* is ECT?'

He puts the glass back on the table.

'Well, electroconvulsive therapy, as the name suggests, produces a convulsion, a *grand mal* convulsion, or in other words, an epileptic fit that lasts but a few seconds. The patient goes into a coma, and again this is only for a moment or two. Then, a period of deep sleep follows. When the patient wakes up there is a gap in their comprehension. This is nothing to worry about. I repeat, this is nothing to worry about.'

He spreads his hands wide to encompass them all, stands up and walks a few paces to the right and then back to the left.

'How many of you have experienced brief periods of

forgetfulness? Perhaps you're driving home from work one night and you realise that you're heading in the direction of a house where you used to live, or maybe you meet an old friend and can't remember their name?'

His grin is boyish, intended to be self-mocking.

'If you're anything like me,' he continues, 'it becomes a bit of a habit.'

A burst of laughter from up the back becomes a ripple. Dr Beckman presses on.

'We could call that a gap in comprehension, a missed beat, a pause, and that pause is similar to what a patient will experience when waking up after ECT. They'll be confused. They might ask, 'Where am I?' 'Who are you?' Or even 'Who am I?'

He leans forward, his face solemn. He allows himself a momentary glance at the woman in the grey dress. Ah, that's a better expression!

'This confused state is, ladies and gentlemen, an important feature of the treatment. Things must change. The patient fears change. ECT imposes the change from outside.'

He can see that they are listening intently. He allows himself a pause. Someone in the front row coughs, but still he waits, rocking back and forth ever so slightly on his heels. He smiles and carries on.

'It's not a drug, therefore it is not addictive. It is administered under medical supervision, and we monitor each patient daily.'

He softens his voice to an almost intimate tone.

'I want the very best for my patients, and I know that what is being done for them, right now, here in this hospital, is for their own good. Thank you.'

The woman in the grey dress has her hand up. Dr Beckman acts as though he hasn't noticed. Already he is turning to Dr Keller, acknowledging with a pursing of his lips and an accompanying brief nod of his head that he is finished.

Dr Keller steps forward.

'Thank you, Dr Beckman . . .'

Someone up the back starts to clap, but Dr Keller holds up his hand.

'I'm aware that time is getting on. Thank you, all of you, for coming. I'm sorry the hospital budget doesn't run to cake or fancy biscuits, but if you'd like to move now to the next room along the hall, members of our catering staff are waiting there to serve you tea and coffee, and, of course, any of us will be happy to answer any further questions you might want to ask.'

John decides not to wait. He hurries out to his car, suddenly aware how dark it is in the hospital grounds. He is pleased he came. He had no idea ECT was such a simple process.

Lights flash behind her eyes, and she keeps hearing funny noises that make her jump with fright. She makes a mess on the floor. The nurses have to clean it up. Nurse Tasker is furious.

'If you do that again, Madeleine Roberts, I'll rub your nose in it.'

In a voice that wobbles and wavers, Madeleine manages to ask a question.

'Is it . . . the . . . the treatment that's doing it?'

Nurse Tasker flashes a haughty look.

'You're letting your imagination run riot, my girl. Now, stop this silly nonsense!'

Determined to stay awake, Madeleine pulls the coffee table into the centre of the day-room floor. If she walks four lengths one side and four lengths the other, she can keep a running tally.

Her thoughts are like discreet conversations whispered too far away to hear. There is something she wants to remember but it slips away, leaving behind a haunting sense of loss. She has to keep counting, but thirty is as far as she can go. Any further and she loses direction, like walking into a maze.

Someone speaks to her. Madeleine has never seen the man before in her life. She turns her back on him. Words buzz round her face. She giggles. The words remind her of helicopters, tiny helicopters that whizz past with no purpose or direction.

Twenty-five, twenty-six, what comes next? Oh God, what comes next? She has to keep going. Get out of my way. She bumps against the coffee table and can't stop herself from falling.

The floor is solid. If she brings her knees in close to her belly and keeps her forehead down flat, she won't know if anyone is watching. Using both hands, she gropes around for the painting. She touches a pointed edge and pulls it towards her. Slowly she makes her way across the room, pushing the painting ahead of her a few inches at a time. She's heading for the corner nearest the porch entrance. That's a good place. Lily used to sit there sometimes. Abruptly Madeleine stops. Lily? Lily? Maybe she's Lily? Is that what the helicopters said?

Her hair, damp with sweat, sweeps across the floor like a wet mop. Lily. What a name. She doesn't feel like a lily. Never liked them much. Lilies are for funerals. Ah, well, it could have been worse. She could've got stuck with gladioli.

Madeleine's forehead is pressed into the corner. From this angle she can look between her legs and count the chairs on the opposite side of the room. One. Two. Three. Four. Maybe, if she stays here long enough, they'll find her doubled over and bent out of shape. Stiff with rigor mortis. Would they break her bones to make her fit in a coffin? Who cares?

I'll meet you in the corner,
like little Jackie Horner,
only I haven't got a plum,
so you'll have to make do with my bum.

Madeleine shrieks with laughter. Urine dribbles onto the floor.

PART 2

Still Counting

Still Counting

The dream is the same night after night. She wakes, and the first thing she notices is the weakness in her legs. Someone is after her. His face is a shadowy mask, but a threat rises from his body like steam. She is preparing to flee, but her legs won't move. They seem paralysed. He's getting closer. For Christ's sake, run! I can't. You must. I can't. I can't.

She lies in the double bed, breathing heavily. Where is she? What is this place? Who is lying next to her?

Her legs are so trembly she doubts she could stand up. She must think.

She is in this room in the dark. Is it a hospital? No, it can't be. Breathe in, then let it out. Her name slowly dawns. She is Madeleine. She is in her own bed in her own home. John is her husband. He is asleep. She has two sons. Flashes of panic claw at her throat. What are their names? Quickly she runs through the alphabet. Adrian, Billy, Carl, no, not Carl, Chris, Chris? No, it's Christopher. Yes. Damian, Edward. Her brother is Edward. Edward and Tim. Two brothers and two sons.

Frank. She's got an Uncle Frank, he's probably dead now, she hasn't seen him since . . . since . . . oh, a long time ago, anyway. Graham, Henry, Isaac, Jamie. Ah, Jamie, he's six years old and lives next door. What's a name beginning with K? Never mind, keep going. Lance, Martin. Martin?

No. Nathan, Oliver, Paul, Richard, Steven, Tim. Skip U. What about V? Van Williams. Broad face, lots of freckles. Forget X. Yul. Bald head, fierce-looking. Zachary Scott. Western type, wore a Stetson – never did see his face, he was all hat.

What kind of a mother is she if she can't remember her own child's name? How old is he? She can see a baby boy in her arms, a baby with reddish-gold hair. Is that him, though, or the other one? If they cut her scalp open now, would her brain look like Swiss cheese?

It must be getting on. She can see daylight through the venetians. A familiar churning starts up in her belly, but she knows now there's no machine.

She reaches her hand down to the floor. Her fingers touch the protruding edge of a painting she keeps under her side of the bed. She strokes the thick lines of paint, seeing the whorls of colour in her mind. Jean. Now, there's a name to remember. The grinding in her belly worsens. She squeezes her eyes shut, holds her breath and counts to ten.

She's like a sailor on a rolling ship, lurching all over the deck in a storm. Do sailors long for oblivion like she does? She's no good to anyone like this.

The alarm goes off. She drags herself out of bed. John is on his way to the bathroom. A child calls out from the next room.

'Can I have a drink of milk, Daddy?'

'Ask your mother, Michael. I've gotta get dressed.'

Michael. Of course. She brings the milk in a mug and kneels beside the bed while he drinks it. Michael. Michael. Please forgive me. Please forgive me.

Huge jagged sections of broken glass, angles pointed danger-ously, are crashing round me like giant spears. I run this way and that trying to avoid being hit. The noise is horrific. Tinny, shrill. I can smell blood and shit. I want to scream, but no human voice could penetrate the din.

Hastily I retreat to a far corner. Now I'm sitting on the floor, my feet pulled in tight. I move my arms to encircle my knees and notice slivers of glass protruding from my wrists. There must be ten or more in each wrist. They're shaped like lightning bolts, stark, strange, beautiful.

They are twinkling flashes of light, reflecting the bright red blood dribbling across my skin and onto the floor. I am a river, flowing beyond the boundaries of flesh in search of the sea.

The plastic doors fly open. Two ambulance officers, one either side of the trolley, run with it down the corridor. A nurse holds back a curtain and ushers them into a cubicle.

'This the suicide?'

'Yeah. One wrist. We've strapped it, but I reckon it's gonna need a lot of stitches.'

He hands her a slip of paper.

'Here's her name. The husband followed us in his car. We didn't wait around for the paperwork, so I'll check the details with you later on. Right, Jim, let's shift her onto the bed.'

They lift the unconscious woman, careful not to touch the arm, which has been slit almost to the elbow. The sheet covering her catches on the side of the trolley and falls away. The woman's clothes are saturated with blood.

'Jesus bloody Christ, what a mess.'

Jim winks at the nurse. 'Not a pretty sight, is she? Her husband reckons she used his Stanley knife.'

The nurse is feeling for a pulse.

'Yeah, and I've just had me dinner.'

'What was it, love? Meat pie and tomato sauce?'

The nurse pokes out her tongue in reply. She lifts the woman's eyelids and begins to slap her face.

'Mrs Roberts, can you hear me?'

Rydalmere. Another hospital. A new psychiatrist. Dr Kemble visits Madeleine in one of two tiny rooms positioned along a veranda with several doors. She's been in the room for about an hour. Her left arm, suspended in the air now by a metal cradle contraption that stands alongside the bed, was stitched early this morning under anaesthetic.

Beneath the dull need for sleep Madeleine is aware of a yawning abyss stretching all around her, keeping her apart from other people. She sees herself walking barefoot around the edge of a rumbling volcano, slipping here and there on sharp stony edges that rip open the skin on her feet and legs. She feels dizzy and frightened, worried that she might fall into that steaming, hissing pit. There's a machine at the core of the volcano, but maybe it isn't a machine? Maybe it's a time-bomb? She wants to yell until her throat is sore, but privately she believes she's beyond help.

Dr Kemble sits near the end of the bed, one leg stretched out like a clothesline prop. He sorts through the bundle of files he's carrying, selects one and places it on top.

'I've had your file sent over from Parramatta, Madeleine, so I already know a little about you.'

He places one finger against an open page.

'It says here you were discharged back in March. That's close on ten months. Quite a long time. Have you coped well during that period?'

Madeleine imagines herself shouting across the abyss.

'Sort of.'

'You kept your appointments with Dr Beckman?'

'Yes.'

'How often did you see him?'

'Once a fortnight.'

'Has anyone explained why you were brought here?'

Madeleine stands on the edge of the volcano, one bloody foot resting on a flat rock. She glances briefly at her slit wrist.

'I thought it was because of this.'

Dr Kemble laughs.

'No. We take all types in both hospitals, but early this year the catchment areas were changed. You live in the Liverpool area, so from now on you must come here.'

Madeleine slips and lands heavily on the flat rock.

'But I was seeing Dr Beckman, why didn't he . . .'

'He was probably hoping you wouldn't have to be admitted again.'

Dr Kemble makes himself more comfortable, leans back, crosses his arms and smiles at Madeleine as though they're old friends.

'Do you mind telling me why you tried to kill yourself?'

Madeleine gets up and stumbles a few paces along the rocks, rubbing her bruised thigh. She has to work hard to keep her balance.

'I . . . we had a row.'

'A row? Your husband said you ran out of the house and

locked yourself in the laundry. Were you trying to draw attention to yourself?'

The edge of the volcano dissolves into fog. She must not move. Stay still. Stay perfectly still.

Stubbornness? Is that what he can see in the set of her jaw?

'I want . . . ed to die.'

'What about your boys? Don't they deserve a mother?'

Madeleine closes her eyes and retreats into the fog.

She wakes with a start. Forgetting, she makes a move to throw back the sheet and jars her hand against its cradle. Pain runs on a straight line in the direction of her heart. She gasps and clenches her teeth to stop herself from screaming.

She hears the sound again. A heavy knock against the wall. A strangled cry is interrupted by a second knock, louder this time. A door opens and closes. Madeleine hears another voice.

'Patients are trying to sleep, Jean. I know your throat is sore, but you must keep calm.'

The strangled cry is longer this time.

'I'll give you a couple of painkillers, but if you throw yourself around like this again I'll have to give you an injection.'

Madeleine lies on her bed in the dark and listens for a reply. The only sound she hears is the closing of a door.

The veranda is wide and runs the length of the building. French doors open onto an asphalt path. Daylight casts an uneven line of mottled shadows on green linoleum, an odd assortment of kitchen chairs, a few tables and a black-and-white television set that flickers a message of wavy lines across the face of a game-show host. Madeleine can just see that he's pointing at a stack of prizes.

She sits on a chair with her cradle contraption beside her, anxious and disturbed by the lack of suitable items to count. She has already counted six doors and thirty-six windows. Each window has ten glass slats that open and close on a metal frame. Louvre windows, the type they used to have in the toilets at school. Three hundred and sixty dirt-speckled louvres.

At Parramatta Hospital there were forty-two chairs in the day-room; here there are thirty-three and five big, round tables. What else? Nothing much. The wall opposite the windows is made of solid brick, but it's been painted over. She tried counting one row across, but it gave her a headache.

What choice is there but people? But hang on – she could have one list for patients and another for nurses. Hmm, how would that work? The TV set is about halfway, so each time someone goes past she can count that as a whole number. The tricky thing is to keep each list separate. What if she gets confused? No. She won't worry about that – after all, she's got nothing better to do.

Nurses forty-one, patients twenty-seven. Twenty-seven, twenty-seven. No. Yes. Twenty-eight. No, she didn't go past the TV, so that doesn't count.

'Watcha do to your arm?'

'What?' *Forty-one, twenty-seven, forty-one, twenty-seven, go away, can't you see I'm busy?*

'I asked you about your arm.'

'I cut it.'

'Oh, yeah, we know all about that.'

'Then why did you ask?'

'I wanted to hear what you'd say.'

Forty-one, twenty-seven. Madeleine turns to look at the woman who has flung herself into a nearby chair. Forty-one, twenty-seven, forty-one, twenty-seven.

'What's your name?'

'Madeleine. What's yours?'

'Fran. You from Parramatta, Madeleine?'

'Yeah.' *Forty-one, twenty-seven.*

'Me too. So's Jean.'

Fran waves a hitchhiker's thumb.

Abandoning her efforts to concentrate, Madeleine searches Fran's face with keen interest.

'Do you know her? Is she the Jean who paints?'

'That's right, she does.'

'What happened to her?'

Fran takes a long puff on her fag before answering.

'She borrowed a dollar from one patient and gave it to another to buy her some razor blades. They reckon she stole a hammer thing from the dispensary and ground up the razor blades till the pieces were small enough to swallow.'

Madeleine winces.

Fran pulls a face and shakes her head. She ignores the long head of ash growing on the end of her cigarette.

'Makes you feel sick, don't it?'

'God, yes. Poor Jean.'

'You know, she'd been trying to get out of Parramatta for years. I haven't found out how she did it, but apparently she ran away. Some bastard up north turned her in to the police. She must have made a nuisance of herself or something – or maybe she stole his wallet?'

Fran flashes an evil grin. She knows whose side she's on.

'Anyway, it didn't take them long to figure out where she came from.'

Madeleine looks around, checking to see if anyone is listening. When she speaks her voice is a soft whisper.

'I remember how she never seemed to be afraid of anyone. Not the nurses or the doctors, nobody.'

Fran's grin is rueful now.

'Not like the rest of us, huh?'

....

There's a male ward along the veranda, separated from the women by a thin partition wall. Nurse Quigley directs Madeleine to the tenth bed in a row of twelve, not far from the toilet door. Madeleine is surprised to hear men's voices. Everything is so different here.

The end wall of Ward 5 has been fitted with a window large enough to cover the width of three beds, including the distance between each one. Nursing staff in the room next door can use this window to see what's going on. It takes Madeleine a while to realise the ward is so long that their view is limited to the small area nearest the veranda door.

Nine o'clock is lock-up time. The key is old, almost an antique. It turns with a heavy, flat sound. Madeleine feels a flutter of panic.

'See you at 6 a.m., ladies. Sleep tight, now.'

....

Beryl's days are full. Clicketty click, clicketty clacketty click. The tips of her steel knitting needles dart back and forth, stabbing the air furiously as the minced-up mash of her mind passes through.

The continuous line of finished pieces gathers in a messy pile at Beryl's feet. It resembles an endless string of brightly coloured sausages — fan-shaped for tea-cosies, squares and oblongs for face washers, all linked in a woolly chain by a single knotted thread.

As Beryl knits, clicketty click, clicketty clacketty click, she softly mumbles the same seven words over and over again: 'The-devil-finds-work-for-idle-hands-the-devil-finds-work-for-idle-hands-the-devil . . .'

At night, under cover of darkness, her hands twitch and shake. Much as she tries to keep them on top of the bed-clothes and away from temptation, her efforts are in vain. The devil has his way with her almost every night, guiding her fingers to stroke here, rub there, yes, that's it, right there, harder, harder, faster, faster until groans of ecstatic pleasure burst out of Beryl's mouth like a crush of canaries, released without warning from a dark, cramped cage.

The darkness is alive in the abrupt silence that follows, as though every woman in the ward has been listening with bated breath.

When Beryl's panting ceases, a wave of disapproval rises up to wash over each bed. But, amidst the tut-tutting and the impatient sighs, a few lie quietly in their beds, a tell-tale smile hovering around their lips. These women are remembering times past, remembering their own cries of pleasure. Secretly they are in awe of Beryl.

In the anonymous darkness, protective and private, they allow their fingers to slide down bare flesh, a tiny gesture of defiance, stopping short of pleasure but lingering for a moment or two in moist regret.

....

'Does your husband remind you of anyone, Madeleine? A brother, your father, an uncle, anyone?'

Dr Kemble detects anger in Madeleine's eyes at the

mention of father, then in an instant the shutters come down and all he's left to look at is the top of her lowered head.

'Tell me about your father.'

'What's there to tell?'

'I don't know. I'm asking you. Were you close?'

'No.'

'Never?'

'Never.'

Her voice is firm. No doubt about her meaning.

'Did you love him?'

Mental gears shift. Her belly grinds into action. Clank, clank. Helpless strands of nausea. For God's sake, put an answer to the question. Play the game. Say something. But I did not know him, that man, my father. I don't understand the question. Why didn't he, I mean why, shouldn't the question be . . . why didn't he love me?

'I don't know.'

Dr Kemble strokes his chin for a brief instant, then plunges into the undergrowth.

'You hated your father, then?'

Hate. Hate. What is hate? The opposite of love? But what is love? Questions. All these questions. Yes. No. Black and white. Draw a line. Make it clear. Hate. Love. Love and marriage. Did my mother and father love each other? Why did it get called love anyway, when it was more like . . . enemies? Why? Black and white. White and black. The descriptions never fit the labels. Dull brain, grey matter. But black and white together is grey, isn't it?

Dr Kemble pauses. That's enough for today. He notes, with some satisfaction, the tears Madeleine seems determined to hide. He closes the door behind her, whistling tunelessly. Yes, he's on to something now. She's more in touch with what's going on around her than she was a month ago.

....

My best friend Kay got a spanking new bike for Christmas the year we both turned ten. It was a bright blue Speedwell with a black leather seat and pink and blue dress-strings over the back wheel. Kay was a generous friend. She allowed me to ride her bike whenever I wanted. Throughout the summer holidays we blackened the tyres with boot polish, softened the leather seat with a mixture of vinegar and linseed oil, wiped all around the spokes with a damp cloth, and flicked imaginary dust from the dress-strings. Once we were satisfied we'd done a good job, we took it in turns to ride up and down our street.

One Sunday afternoon, when Kay and her mother had gone to visit friends, I walked up the back lane that ran past both our houses, opened the gate into Kay's back yard and wheeled her bike down the lane and into a street further away from home. My sister Lizzie was waiting near the brick fence in front of a large block of flats.

Though Lizzie was older than me, she had never learnt to ride, so I'd promised I would teach her on Kay's bike. Pushing the bike between us, we headed up the hill. We passed a black car parked close to the kerb. I was pleased there was only one car. Just then a man came out of the flats carrying a bucket of water.

At the top of the hill we turned into a dead-end street. There were few houses here, and Lizzie and I had agreed this was a good place for our purpose. Lizzie climbed onto the seat, using my shoulder for support. I held on to the handlebars with one hand and the back of the seat with the other. In this awkward fashion we went back and forth, making a wide circle at each end of the tiny street so that Lizzie didn't have to get off.

My plan was to wait till I thought she was confident enough for me to let go. When that moment came, I'd wait until we were facing away from the dead-end, give the bike a push and send Lizzie down the hill. I was convinced her common sense would take over and she would find her balance as quick as a wink. Besides, there was always the back-pedal brake if she needed it.

Judging the moment to be right, I let go of the handlebars and pushed the seat out of my grasp, careful that my forward thrust did not tip the bike to either side. I watched Lizzie shoot round the corner and proceed down the hill, exactly as I'd planned. She didn't scream, and I thought that was a good sign. The front wheel wobbled, but she was still upright. I shouted encouragement and ran to catch up.

Despite the good start, Lizzie seemed to have forgotten all about steering and was heading right for the parked car. I could see the man swirling his chamois in a soapy lather on the car roof. He was so preoccupied that he didn't notice anything until the bike hit the back bumper-bar and thudded over to one side, throwing Lizzie over the handlebars and across the roof. I saw the man jump backwards, saw the shocked look on his face. The soapy water must have added to Lizzie's momentum. She shot forward into thin air. I was running so fast I saw everything happen right before my eyes like a slow-motion film, yet it was all over in a matter of seconds.

The car's mascot was an elaborate specimen of highly polished chrome with a dangerous spiky point. If Lizzie had landed on that it would have made a terrible mess. I remember thinking about this as I leant over her. She was lying in a crumpled heap. For one split second I thought she might be dead.

How could things go wrong so quickly?

The man was shouting at us, but nothing he said made any sense. He could have been screaming at us from across the

Queensland border for all I cared. Oh, God, if you're there, please listen. I promise I won't do anything like this ever again. Please let this day be over and let everything be all right. If Mum finds out, we'll really cop it.

By now he was red in the face. He kept opening his mouth and closing it again and shaking his fist at us menacingly. My sister was hurt, and all he could do was carry on about his precious car. What if she'd been killed? It was all my fault.

I helped her to get up. She was doubled over and groaning, but I could tell she was as anxious as I was to get away. She managed to walk, a few steps at a time, both arms clenched firmly around her belly. I hurried back to get the bike, half dragging, half carrying it along the street. The man didn't try to stop us. I think he must still have been suffering from shock. When we got to our back gate Lizzie sank to the ground and I continued up the lane. Oh, God, let me get the bike back to Kay's place without anyone seeing me, please, God, just this once.

The front wheel was buckled and the frame was badly twisted. There were deep scratches in several places. I pushed open the gate and pulled the bike through after me. I was fearful of making a noise. Georgina, Kay's older sister, later said she saw me from the kitchen window but thought nothing of it till that evening when she saw the state of the bike.

Back in the lane Lizzie was leaning against the fence, trying not to cry. I helped her inside. She had a nasty graze right across her stomach. Bits of skin hung loose in two places, and lower down there were red marks and the beginnings of a bruise. Both her elbows had been split open and there was a nasty gash on her right knee. We tore up an old school blouse for bandages. It was white, and hopefully wouldn't be missed. I hunted around for something she could wear that wouldn't rub against her belly.

We didn't talk about it all being my fault. We were too intent on staying out of trouble. I didn't think twice about lying; it was a matter of priorities. I was scared. Scared of my mother and even more scared of my father. They mustn't find out. Whatever Kay and her family thought about us was no concern of mine — not yet, anyway.

There was a knock on our front door that night. Lizzie and I were doing the washing up. We didn't dare look at each other. I felt hot and clammy and my legs were suddenly weak. When Mum called us, I wondered if I'd make it down the hallway. Lizzie stood alongside me, feigning surprise at Mum's questions. We recounted our activities for the whole afternoon. We'd cleaned our room, brought in the washing and peeled the potatoes for tea. It was all true, but we'd done these chores after the accident.

I didn't realise it then, but Mum wasn't really interested in working out how we'd spent our time. If we'd owned up she'd have been responsible. Kay's family might even have demanded a new bike. It was unusual for Mum to take our side. I think she knew all along we were lying.

Kay and Georgina had little choice but to walk away. Kay was crying. I knew our friendship was over. Who needed friends anyhow?

....

Nella waits for the sound of the key turning in the lock. On nights like tonight, it's her own secret signal. Satisfied all is quiet, she rises from her bed, brisk with energy. Her eyes are no longer dull and blank but gleaming with purpose. She has green eyes like a cat, and she can see in the dark.

Nella has never told a living soul that she's been singled out. God has chosen her to expiate her sins here on earth, and when she dies, in the name of the Father, Son and Holy Ghost, He has promised she'll go straight to heaven. Few could understand what all this means. Even Nella has trouble with the idea at times.

Armed with a bucket, a mop and various items of under-wear – her own and anyone else's she can lay hands on – to use as cloths, she goes forth to clean the toilet block, not once, not twice, but five times over till at last she is given permission to return to her bed.

There is a method, a dutiful sense of order, imposed on Nella's punishment. God will almost certainly destroy her with radiation rays if she doesn't get it right. Not for a moment does she doubt His word. If killing her with them rays is what He said, that's exactly what He will do, no kidding.

The bucket and mop are kept behind the toilet door near the light switch. The mop isn't very good, and Nella wishes she could buy her own, but she is consoled by the bucket. It is made of metal, and there's a foot lever on the side. Right foot, mind, always the right, never ever the left. That would be asking for much trouble.

Stick the dripping wet mop between the two rollers, press the lever down hard, yes, I mean hard, Nella, and all the water runs into the bucket.

Nella begins quietly, respectful of His presence some-where on the ceiling, but as the hours pass her actions become fierce, her respect overtaken by loud and angry protests. Why does she have to do this? Hasn't she cleaned enough? Six sons and two lazy daughters, what you say to that, God? What you say to me?

The noise of the bucket scraping across the tiled floor in the middle of the night is enough to drive the other patients stark raving mad.

Some of the women in Ward 5 think Nella should be moved to another ward, the sort of ward they imagine is set aside for really disturbed patients. Those on night-time medication breathe audible sighs of relief. Their heads sink deep into their pillows while they wait for the swirling waters of oblivion to pull them under. Some patients moan aloud or mutter tight-lipped complaints, but Nella is too preoccupied to see or hear.

Madeleine tosses and turns. Is this some kind of torture? Nella is a driven woman, sure, but soon they'll all be round the twist. She can hear the swish-swish of the mop, the full-throated curses and the occasional grunt each time Nella has to put in extra effort, but it's the harsh sound of the bucket being shoved along a few inches at a time, probably by Nella's foot, that makes her blood run cold.

Most of what Nella says is incoherent, but the tone of voice is enough to intimidate anyone who even dares to think of intervening in her private torment.

Finally it is over. Nella stumbles about, emptying the last bucket of water, propping the door open with the mop, switching off the light, shuffling across the ward in her sodden slippers. Madeleine knows exactly the moment when Nella plonks herself down on the side of her bed, lies back to the tune of a broken spring and lifts her feet off the floor.

Within seconds, or so it seems to Madeleine, Nella is snoring loudly. Madeleine pounds her pillow in frustration. That is the worst insult of all. It is dawn before she finally drops off to sleep.

Madeleine fixes her attention on a corner of Dr Kemble's desk, tracing a number of tiny scratches with her fingers. Five circular marks. How did they get there? Maybe it was when the desk was moved into this room. Maybe it was a patient, a patient with a knife . . .

'I saw you on my way in this morning.'

She is immediately wary. Is this some kind of trap?

'You were sitting with your back against a tree, staring at the ground.'

How long had he been watching her?

Dr Kemble doesn't smile, but his face takes on a pleading expression.

'What were you doing?'

Relieved suddenly, Madeleine begins to talk. Words spill from her mouth in a steady flow. She is grateful she can talk to him about something.

'I was watching the ants. I could look at them for hours. I guess you could call me an ant-lover. They're so hard-working, and . . .' – she searches for the right words – 'and a happy sort of . . . community.'

'Ants?'

His tone should have warned her, but her mind is still on the ants.

'There's this anthill, see, it's not very big, but there are so many ants and they're all busy-busy. They carry enormous loads – well, enormous when you consider the size of an ant – and and . . .'

His laughter takes her by surprise. She feels his contempt like a blow. He carries on as though she's been telling him some hilarious joke.

'Ants? You were sitting there communing with ants?'

Her face closes up tight. She pulls herself into a small space. Don't move a muscle. Stay perfectly still.

This man frightens her. He makes her feel like a small child, like a tiny ant about to be squashed under his shoe. One, two, I won't look at you. Three, four, eyes on the floor. Five, five, it's no fun being alive.

....

An Indian summer's night. The air is soft and still and full of unexpected heat. Bedclothes have been thrown back, and bodies roll this way and that in search of a cool spot.

Beryl is at it again. Undaunted by the weather, she clings to an illusion of dignity, the top sheet tucked under her chin. Her body rocks and throbs and the iron bed squeaks and creaks a protesting rhythm.

Madeleine is drifting in that space that is not yet sleep but beckons it closer. Roused by the noise, she wonders briefly if Nella is out of bed. Beryl groans, then begins in earnest.

'Oh. Oh. Ohh. Oh. Oh.'

'God, Beryl,' Madeleine sighs in an exhausted whisper, 'wherever do you get your energy?'

....

Nurse Quigley looks at her watch. Two minutes before seven o'clock.

'Come, come, ladies, move along. It's time you were off to get your breakfast. No, Nella, this way. Out. Out.'

The woman in Bed 2 has only been here overnight. She doesn't yet understand the rules.

'What if it's cold later on, Nurse? Can I come back for my cardigan?'

Nurse Quigley is making silent gestures to another

patient, indicating that the woman's bed isn't properly made. She walks over to the newcomer, speaking as though she were reading from a book.

'This ward is locked from 7 a.m. till 8.30 p.m. Anything you might want throughout the day must be taken with you.'

The tone of her voice changes, heavy with sarcasm and a smile to match.

'We don't make the rules round here, but we don't break them either.'

Madeleine mingles with the throng of patients gathered on the veranda, joining the queue heading out the French doors. About to step onto the asphalt path, she spots Jean further along the veranda.

Madeleine pulls away from the door and heads in Jean's direction. Only when she gets closer does she see the spreading red stains on the sleeves of Jean's shirt. Jean is transfixed. She holds her arms out in front, calmly contemplating the blood bubbling up from her wrists. Splashes of blood are falling onto the floor, creating pools and spray patterns.

Madeleine is aware of one or two women close by. Like her, they have been frozen into a strange tableau for several seconds. Jean faints, and that breaks the spell. Fran comes from behind, dropping to her knees, grabbing Jean's wrists, encircling them, pressing the palms of her hands down onto the wounds. Another woman breaks into a run, hurtling headlong down the veranda with a blood-curdling yell as though she were being chased by a madman with an axe. Madeleine calls out for Nurse Quigley, but can't help wondering if Jean would prefer that she didn't.

Within minutes it is as though the incident had never happened. Two nurses have whisked Jean away and a third has brought a bucket of soapy water and a mop.

A few days later Fran finds Madeleine walking round the grounds near the canteen. She gives a shout and comes running over.

'She's out of danger – they reckon she's going to be all right. They're talking about bringing her back here in a day or two.'

Madeleine doesn't reply. She and Fran stand a few feet apart, looking at one another with tears in their eyes. Madeleine reaches a hand out, touches Fran's arm and walks away.

....

Jean is back in her tiny room. Her face is grey with fatigue, and it's obvious that she's lost a lot of weight. Nurse Quigley insists that Jean sit on the veranda for a brief while each morning, and again in the late afternoon.

Madeleine pulls up a chair. 'How are you?'

'I feel so fit I could jump over the moon.' Jean's face takes on a disgusted look. 'What do you think?'

'Did you mean to kill yourself?'

'No. I did it for fun.'

Madeleine stands up and makes a move to walk away.

'Don't go, please.'

Madeleine sits, waiting for Jean to say something more.

'I don't feel any pain, you know. In an odd sort of way, it gives me relief.'

Madeleine nods. 'I know.'

She stretches her arm across the table between them. Jean and Madeleine stare at the long jagged scar on the inside of Madeleine's arm. Jean holds out her bandaged wrists, laying them on the table, palms turned upwards, one either side of Madeleine's arm.

'My turn.'

Jean is wearing a sleeveless nightshirt. Her arms are thin and sprinkled with freckles. Madeleine inspects the scars that run, in varying lengths, from above the bandaged wrists to Jean's shoulders. In some places old scars have been criss-crossed by further cuts. Madeleine enquires about an ugly welt near Jean's elbow. She touches it lightly with her finger.

'This one. How did you do it?'

'I used a broken bottle then I opened it up further with a piece of tin.'

Madeleine assumes a mock scowl.

'Rusty tin, of course,' she says.

'Of course. I never did like short sleeves anyway.'

They laugh companionably. Jean touches Madelaine's arm with her fingertips. 'D'you know why they put these places near the water?' she asks.

'No,' Madeleine says. 'Why?'

'Well, they say, back in the early days, that lunatics weren't allowed to travel on the King's highway, so they had to be ferried around by boat. The asylums were all built on the rivers or near the harbour. I s'pose they took the bodies out the same way.'

Madelcine shivers, remembering Lily.

They hear Nurse Quigley's voice before they see her. She is striding down the veranda barking out instructions left and right.

'Move away from that TV, John, you're sitting too close. Beryl, get that knitting out of the way before someone trips over it and breaks their neck.'

Madeleine hastens away from the table and Jean stares off into space.

Around lunchtime the next day a nurse finds Jean slumped in a messy heap at the back of the canteen. This time it is too late. Jean is dead. No one tells the patients in Ward 5, but it doesn't take long for Fran to find out.

That night in bed Madeleine hugs Jean's painting to her chest. She can't stop crying.

Visiting graves was an obsession in my mother's family. During the 1940s and '50s, my mother and various aunts would traipse across Sydney, sometimes waiting for ages on a Sunday for a bus, tram or train, sticking to the yearly schedule with a determined passion that never waned. Husbands were not expected to attend — this was family business — but woe betide the man who tried to stop them.

Mother's Day was extra special. I remember getting up early for the trek to Waverley cemetery to put flowers on my grandmother's grave. My mother bought the biggest bunch of chrysanthemums she could afford. It was a matter of pride and honour — the bigger the bunch, the greater the proof of what a good daughter you were.

Mum got off the tram at Bronte, clutching her huge bunch of chrysanthemums in front of her like a holy relic, every step she took solemn and dignified, as though she were taking part in a religious procession. My sister Lizzie and I would bring up the rear, carrying freshly washed jam jars and a posy of flowers picked from next door's garden.

I'd be hoping Mrs Benson wouldn't know I'd stolen the sweet-smelling rose that just yesterday had been blooming, full-faced, near her front gate; and would she miss the snapdragons I'd grabbed from the thick clump that grew close to the fence on our side?

At the main gate we'd meet up with Mum's sisters. Kitty and Jessie were always there. Winnie had been ill for years but she did her best to make it. The other eight lived in far-flung places across the State and took it in turns every five years. Mum would proceed down the path towards the sea, kids running ahead in search of Nanna's grave.

Once we'd said our hellos to Nanna, I'd be sent to fill the jam jars at the nearest tap. I had to walk back carefully to avoid the water slopping over. The ground was uneven and dipped unexpectedly between one row of graves and the next.

After great deliberation, vases of flowers were placed along the length of the grave, then the sisters passed old photos of their mother back and forth. Looking at the frail woman staring back at me, I would worry about all that dirt. Did the headstone press too hard on her forehead? Was she strong enough to push the slab of marble and all those little white stones out of her way?

My grandmother died long before I was born, but I liked to think of her sitting up after we'd gone, catching a glimpse of blue ocean and commenting aloud to herself about the lovely flowers. I hoped she'd know who'd brought the snapdragons and the sweet-smelling rose.

During the times when my mother wasn't visiting graves, she'd read the death notices every day without fail, and she was always keen to know who was walking about on tottering legs.

'He's on his last,' she'd say, pointing out some unfortunate neighbour.

She planned her funeral with elaborate detail, giving her children regular updates about her preferred hymns and what sort of flowers she wanted. She'd joined a funeral fund in her early thirties, and every week she paid a small sum for expenses and a burial plot. She spent hours writing lists of people who would have to be invited personally, and when her children grew up her conversations with them were sprinkled with threats about whether or not they would be allowed to attend.

'I'm going to pretend I never did have a daughter named Madeleine,' she'd warn, narrowing her lips to show that this was serious, that a deep rift had opened up in her heart.

Her threats became like a game of musical chairs.

'I'm cutting you out of my will . . .'

Tim, Lizzie, Madeleine, Edward. Whoever was guilty of something that week. Behind her back it became a joke we shared.

'You in the will?'

'I think so, but I haven't seen her this week, so maybe not.'

'What's she got to leave, anyway?'

'You haven't seen the list? Well, there's a twin-tub washing machine, a ghastly carved ashtray on a stand, three Al Jolson records and . . .'

'. . . I know, the final payment on the funeral fund.'

'How did you guess?'

I still wonder about my mother's morbid interest in her own death. It was her big moment. Fifteen minutes of fame, an event that had to be prepared for in plenty of time. And what about Jean? Was her desperation — and mine — born of a need to obliterate the present, to have life over and done with? A cry for help or a pain so urgent, so overwhelming, that all you can do is try to make it end, now, right this minute, with a full stop. Nothing matters after that. Is Jean out there somewhere, desperate with longing for another chance? I don't think so.

In a large room close to the building that houses Ward 5, seventy-two patients and five nurses assemble in a wide semi-circle. Beryl has pulled her chair over near the door and is knitting furiously. Two male patients take up positions at the back of the room, standing motionless in opposite corners, like museum exhibits. Nella paces back and forth. She is mumbling incoherently and pulling faces. Other patients fidget and squirm in their seats. Facing them astride his chair, forearms crossed and resting along its back, is the Head Nurse, Dougal Fricker.

Dougal complains about untidiness. Wards are not pigsties. Patients have to behave properly, like they would in their own bedrooms at home. They must take better care of their things. And their behaviour at meals is disgusting. Haven't they ever been taught to use a knife and fork properly?

Halfway through the allotted hour, he changes his approach. His smile becomes a meandering butterfly that comes to rest on one of the long-term patients sitting in the second row. Ah, Joseph. Dougal announces that from now on the new Ward President will help to chair these weekly meetings, and must also look after the badminton racquets and the pool cues and balls. Joseph looks from left to right. He does not yet understand the honour that has been bestowed upon him.

Next Dougal reads from a list of names. These patients have expressed concern about their medication. He asks questions, but tightens his lips to show impatience if the answers aren't expressed in a simple yes or no. He produces a small notepad and pen and jots down the odd note, promising to look up files or consult Dr Kemble if he thinks that's necessary. At last he puts his pen back in his pocket. It is clear the meeting is about to end.

Jimmy has had his hand up for a while. Dougal acknowledges him with a resigned sigh.

'All right, Jimmy, I know what you're going to say. I don't

know why you want to bring it up here, but I guess you won't be happy till everyone hears your little tale of woe.'

Jimmy stands up and adopts a respectful stance, tucking his shirt into his trousers, then running his fingers around the inside of his collar. He coughs once or twice to ease his nervousness.

'Ah, Mr Fricker, sir, I've been asking for weeks now. Can I please go see my wife's . . .'

Dougal's eyes flash with irritation.

'And I've told you, Jimmy, again and again, it's no use asking till you've got a decent outfit to wear. Look at yourself—you're a damned disgrace. You look like you're ready to go walkabout.'

Jimmy opens his mouth to say something but thinks better of it. He sits down, head and shoulders hunched over, his gaze fixed on the square of linoleum between his boots.

When the meeting ends, he's first out the door.

....

Jimmy's always been a jovial type of bloke. Ask him what he wants out of life and he'll tell you right off—a joke, a good woman and a tall glass of beer. That is, he used to say that. Now look at him. He seldom laughs, the good woman is dead, and no matter how much beer he drinks it's never enough to damp down the pain. Not that he's got money to drown his sorrows, but there's usually someone who doesn't like to drink alone, who'll shout him a drink.

Jimmy walks through the grounds of Rydalmere Hospital on his way back from the pub. He can walk a straight line or even jump over that bench there. See?

Strolling past the canteen, he hears his name called. One of the women from Ward 5 is coming out the door.

He waves, about to walk on.

'Hey, Jimmy, wait up.'

She comes over, clutching a tube of toothpaste and a cellophane packet that she's tearing open with her teeth. She holds out the bag of barley sugar.

'Want one?'

'No, ta. I'm sucking on a peppermint.'

He opens his mouth to show a half-sucked lolly.

Madeleine unwraps a barley sugar and holds it in place with two fingers, above her outstretched tongue.

'Do you think they'd let us enter the egg-and-spoon race?'

She laughs self-consciously at her slurred speech.

Jimmy replies with a short-lived smile.

'Not funny, huh?'

'Sorry.'

This time his smile is more genuine.

Madeleine falls into line with his loping stride, skipping every few steps to keep up.

'Listen, I hope I don't sound like I'm sticking my nose into your private business, but what does Fricker mean when he says you can't see your wife?'

Madeleine has to lean sideways to hear the whispered reply.

'My wife is dead. They won't let me visit her grave till I get some proper clothes.'

Madeleine can't comprehend what he is saying.

'What sort of clothes? What difference do your clothes make?'

He turns his head in Madeleine's direction, but his eyes focus on a point some distance away.

'You married?'

'Yes, I am.'

'Kids?'

'Yes.'

'Alice wanted a girl.'

Tears stream down his face. He drops to the ground and begins to sob. Madeleine doesn't know what to do. Should she go for help? Is he all right? Stupid bloody questions. Now look what she's done.

The sobs end abruptly. Jimmy gets to his feet.

'This is no place to cry,' he mutters.

'I know what you mean,' she replies helplessly.

They walk back to the ward in silence.

Fran hangs around the canteen, hoping for a windfall, a stroke of luck.

'Hey, Franky, buy us a Coke, will ya?'

'Doc-tor Kem-ble says I'm n-ot to gi-ve an-y mo-ney a-way . . .'

Fran moves in closer and throws her arm around his shoulders.

'But he didn't mean me, Franky. We're mates, you and me, mates is differ . . .'

A nurse comes striding along and takes in the scene at a glance.

'Piss off, you, and leave him alone.'

'Where've you been?'

'I just told you, up the pub. You oughta come some time.'

Fran's happy grin is quickly replaced by a frown.

'Don't look so shocked, Madeleine. We're not robbing banks or nothing.'

'It isn't that. I thought – I mean, aren't we supposed to stay in the grounds? Isn't there a rule about it?'

Mollified by Madeleine's confusion, Fran explains.

'Only for some patients, but they're locked up anyway. As for the rest of us . . .'

She arches her eyebrows and throws her head back slightly.

'. . . well, we just have to make our own fun.'

Madeleine begins to laugh. It's a strange, tormented sound that goes on and on. Fran joins in, uncertain what the joke is but willing to oblige. She grabs Madeleine's hands, and together they spin round and round.

They collapse in a heap on the grass. Madeleine shields her eyes from the late afternoon sun.

'I don't get it. They go to the trouble of locking us up all night, then lock us out all day, and . . . and now I learn they don't give a shit what we do or where we go. Why keep us here at all?'

Fran is busy pulling up blades of grass, rubbing them between her fingers.

'My Dad used to say there's them that makes the rules and them who learn how to get around the rules. That's what I do – life's simpler that way.'

'But don't you want to know why things are done the way they are?'

'What good would it do? Would it change anything? Those bloody doctors and the rest of them in there . . .' She points a thumb in the direction of the hospital buildings. '. . . they're from a different world to us. We're not their sort and they're not ours. I'm not like Jean – I can't fight them, I just keep out of their way.'

Later, in bed, Madeleine can't sleep. Grinding spasms in

her groin make her want to cry. She feels an urge to stick her fingers down her throat in order to heave. But riding below the waves of nausea there are thoughts that keep surfacing. She's tried counting, but the numbers lodge in her mind like dry biscuits in a dry mouth, thick and lumpy obstacles that won't budge. Whimpering sounds rise from her bed. Finally, as the first rays of morning light show through the glass in the veranda door, she drops off, her last waking thought a phantom that struggles to catch her attention.

It isn't the people locked up in institutions that worry me, it's the ones that aren't.

....

Hot, squally winds form eddies of leaves and litter, throwing up gritty specks of dirt into the path of pedestrians, attacking their faces and arms. At a set of traffic lights, Madeleine scurries across the road, a few steps behind a lanky schoolboy in a neat blue uniform. Why isn't he at school?

Inside the pub it's cool. She notices a flower-patterned carpet in shades of red. The wooden chairs are stained a streaky black, with leather insets on the seats held in place by metal studs. The same stained wood has been used for the tables. She stands close to a jukebox, a gaudy specimen with red, green and yellow flashing lights. A record drops onto the turntable and Elvis begins to sing 'Are you lonesome tonight?' Yes, Elvis, I am.

The atmosphere is smoky. Several people are ordering drinks. The bartenders joke with the customers as they place large, foam-topped glasses of beer on the counter and ring up the money in the till. She rushes outside, feeling shaky and panicked.

Square, squat buildings line both sides of Victoria Road —

small factories, most of them. She decides to keep walking. There has to be a milk bar around here somewhere.

The sandwich shop is on a corner, set back some distance from the road. Madeleine climbs onto a stool, one of six bolted to the floor along the length of a high, narrow bench facing the window. It's too early for the lunchtime crowd, so she can sit here for a bit. She sips her coffee and stares at the cars and trucks whizzing past.

'Like my new shirt?'

She spins around, uncertain where the voice is coming from.

The man who made her cappuccino twirls in a slow circle, his arms held high like a dancer, his dark olive complexion shown off to advantage by the creamy-coloured material of his shirt. He comes to a halt near her stool.

'Nice, huh? You like?' Reluctantly Madeleine places her coffee cup back in its saucer. She stares with feigned interest at his shirt.

'Yes, very nice. What is it? Silk?'

'Feel it.'

The man holds out his arm. She folds a small section of the sleeve between her fingertips and rubs its back and forth a few times. She doesn't know what silk is supposed to feel like, not the good stuff anyway, but if she had to guess, she'd say this was the real thing.

'My wife, she say it is silk, very good material, I think.'

'Yes, very good.'

'Want to know where I get it?'

'Yes, of course,' she replies politely.

Over her shoulder he points to a dingy yellow building on the other side of the road. The words 'St Vincent de Paul' are sign-printed in big letters on the shop window.

Madeleine turns back to face him, surprise and delight showing on her face.

'No. Really?'

He glows with pleasure, and soon they're discussing the cost of children's clothes, shoes, even the rising price of a cup of coffee. The man reaches behind the counter and holds up a worn tobacco pouch.

'Cigarettes much much expensive. These days I roll my own.'

To her surprise, Madeleine feels at ease with this man, enough to tell him something about herself.

'It's funny, but I've never taken it up. Most of my friends smoke – I'm the odd one out . . .'

Pausing, she checks the expression on his face. Is he interested? Is he listening? The man nods his head encouragingly and waits for her to continue.

'I did try to take it up . . . I was about eighteen and I tried it for a week, but I . . .'

She interrupts herself with a self-conscious laugh.

'I could never figure out what to do with the cigarette pack and the matches. I was so awkward . . .' Warming to the memory, she giggles. 'And the taste . . .'

She rolls her eyes and screws up her face.

His eyes twinkle with merriment.

'So, now you are a millionaire, yes?'

They laugh like old friends.

'You want another cup of coffee?' he asks. 'My shout, please, I insist.'

An hour later all six stools are occupied, and there is a steady stream of customers waiting in line at the sandwich counter. Madeleine stands in the doorway, determined to catch the man's attention. He looks up from the sandwich he is cutting and waves a breadknife in the air. She waves back and slips out the door.

She crosses the road with a stream of factory workers coming in the other direction, and hurries into the dingy yellow op-shop. Ignoring the racks filled to overflowing with blouses and skirts and dresses, she inspects instead the long row of suits and jackets. She has twenty-two dollars and a few odd coins in her purse. She's prepared to spend the lot if she can find what she's looking for. It doesn't take long. She carries the selected items to the counter.

An elderly woman folds up the dark blue jacket, and together they check that all the silver buttons are sewn on tight. The white shirt has a stiff collar and looks brand new.

'I don't think it's been worn much,' the elderly woman remarks. 'Just look at those cuffs.'

Madeleine hasn't got enough money to pay for the tie.

'I do really want that one. It's a perfect match for the jacket, and my friend has grey trousers . . .'

She drops her voice to a confiding whisper, 'He's going to visit his wife's grave, and I know she'd want him to look nice . . .'

The elderly woman folds the tie and places it on top of the shirt.

'How does twenty dollars for the lot sound?'

With the large plastic bag in one hand she walks along the veranda of Ward 5, searching among the men for someone who can help her carry out her plan.

It's Warren who tells her that Jimmy's bed is the third one from the door, on the right.

'Why do ya wanna know, anyway?'

She has her answer ready.

'I heard a man cry out during the night. I thought it might be Jimmy. I wondered if he was all right.'

'Him? He's OK. Snores like a happy drunk, that one.'

Warren looks at her slyly, and his voice takes on a drawling snigger.

'Mr Fricker won't like it if he hears you're hangin' round with Jimmy Boy.'

Madeleine turns away, pretending she hasn't heard.

Every night around 8.30 p.m. Dougal Fricker unlocks the wards. He begins down the far end with the men's ward, then moves along, unlocking the other two in turn. Tonight he emerges from his office on the dot, a large bunch of keys jingling from the chain attached to his belt.

Most people prefer to keep out of Dougal's way, so there's usually a lull of about five minutes before patients come trailing in. Madeleine has been preparing for this moment all afternoon. Along the veranda several patients, mostly women, are gathered around the television set, but no one is showing any interest in her and Fran.

They've dragged a table as far down the veranda as they dare, and Fran has her eyes trained now on Dougal's departing back.

'Go,' she whispers.

Running softly, Madeleine heads for the men's ward. She pulls the clothes from the plastic bag and lays them out on Jimmy's bed, draping the tie neatly across the front of the shirt. Heart racing, face flushed with excitement, she is back sitting at the table with Fran a minute later.

The two exchange significant glances when they see Jimmy. He is one of the first men to arrive. He disappears into the ward, then hurries out again and looks around. He spies the two women and stands there, hands on his hips, looking at them, a puzzled expression furrowing his brow.

'Did you . . .'

Fran adopts an expression of childlike innocence.

'What's the matter, Jimmy, something up?'

He doesn't reply but looks from one to the other, his face a question mark.

'Something you want to tell us?' Fran asks.

By now he is certain. He draws closer, wary still, but unable to keep his lips from widening into a smile.

Madeleine feels warmly towards this man, aware of their shared helplessness when faced with the stern-faced doctors and people like Douglas Fricker.

She leans in Jimmy's direction.

'Why don't you try them on, and then you can tackle City Slicker Fricker while we're all in a good mood.'

'You reckon?'

'Yeah, go on,' Fran urges. 'I want to see the look on his face.'

A few minutes later, dressed in his finery, Jimmy returns to their table.

'Turn around,' Fran says.

He does as he is told.

'Nice,' Fran murmurs. 'Very nice.'

The jacket fits well across his shoulders. Though it's a little long in the sleeves, the overall effect is dramatic.

'That tie is exactly right,' Fran tells him.

Madeleine notices how Jimmy's blue-black skin gleams above the white collar, and he seems to be standing more erect somehow. He winks at Fran and Madeleine, stoops slightly and crooks both arms, a gentlemanly invitation.

Flanked by Fran and Madeleine, he saunters along the veranda in the direction of Dougal Fricker's office.

....

One week later a stranger comes to Ward 5, a tall woman in a flowing skirt and brown leather boots. She has Jimmy's name written down in a little book. They drive away in her pale-blue car. Fran and Madeleine are there to wave him off. Embarrassed in front of the stranger, Fran waits until Jimmy is sitting in the car before thrusting a small packet of tissues in his hands.

'Just in case you feel like bawling,' she says.

'Did you get us a packet too?' Madeleine asks as they watch the car drive out of the hospital grounds.

....

Dougal Fricker writes a memo to Dr Kemble. Two days later Madeleine is summoned to Dr Kemble's office. He greets her with a broad smile.

'I've spoken to your husband this morning, Madeleine, and guess what? We've decided you can go home for the weekend.'

He sits on the edge of his desk, one hand lightly resting on the back of her chair.

'Prove to us you can cope, and we may be able to discharge you quite soon.'

She waits on the veranda for John. Her bag is packed, and she has offered to take home a load of washing for Jimmy.

'You're sure you don't mind?' he asks for the umpteenth time.

'Of course not. It's only a matter of bunging the clothes in the machine.'

'As long as you're sure.'

'I'm sure, I'm sure.'

She punches him lightly on the arm. That beaten-down look has gone from his face, and earlier this morning he talked about a trip out west.

'I want to go home and see Mum,' he explained, chewing on a piece of toast. 'She's a good woman, my Mum. I can talk things over with her, decide what I'm going to do.'

Maybe we'll be discharged about the same time, Madeleine is thinking, watching John walk across the grass and in through the door.

She's been home an hour, and already it feels like the time away has been nothing more than a bad dream. She insists John's mother sit down and put her feet up while she organises lunch.

Back and forth between the kitchen bench and the table she carries plates, cutlery, bowls of lettuce, tomato, thin slices of Devon sausage and fresh bread rolls bought on the way home. Christopher sits astride her hip. He cries if she tries to put him down. She has to keep moving him from one side to the other – he's too big to carry and she's not used to his weight. She lowers him to the height of the table so he can put the tub of margarine down all by himself.

Michael is playing on the floor. Madeleine watches him move the row of Matchbox cars forward, one inch at a time. He looks up occasionally, his eyes solemn, his head on one side.

'Do you like your new truck?' she asks, her face as serious as his own. When Michael was born, Madeleine had the eerie sense of an old, old, soul peering up at her from this tiny baby's eyes. She still feels reluctant to disturb the space around him, unwilling to intrude.

'Yes thank you.'

He inspects the yellow truck carefully before setting it in place at the end of the row.

'Brmmm, brmmm.'

After lunch she puts a sleepy Christopher down on the lounge. Now she can tackle the washing. The first load is done. She carries the basket of wet clothes to the line. John has finished mowing. He wheels the mower closer to the house and reaches for the hose.

'Those white socks, they're not mine, are they?'

'No, they belong to Jimmy – you remember I introduced you to him?'

'So why are you doing his bloody washing?'

'Because his wife is dead and he hasn't got anyone else.'

'Can't he do it himself?'

Madeleine grits her teeth.

'I'm doing him a very small favour, John, that's all.'

He tosses the hose down. It thrashes around like an angry snake. John takes his time switching off the tap. Pools of water form on the cement path. Holding the now-empty basket, Madeleine accidentally steps into a coil of hose just as John pulls sharply further along its length. She jumps out of the way, about to protest, when she notices that he is glaring at her. She responds with head-drooping silence. Taut wires of tension stretch across the narrow space between them. The moment hovers, then moves on. John hauls in the hose, and Madeleine heads for the laundry.

She's been under the shower a long time. She comes out of the bathroom, switches off the light and walks into the hallway. John and his mother are still sitting at the kitchen table, nursing mugs of tea. Their voices drop as she approaches.

'The pot's still warm. I'll pour you some,' Iris says, jumping up hurriedly, glad to have something to do.

'It's all right, thanks, I want to check the washing. I'll have a cup later.'

Madeleine brings the basket of washing inside. She folds each item with practised speed, creating several neat piles.

Iris sits upright in her chair, bracing herself.

'I do think John's right, you know. It doesn't do to give people the wrong idea. They can take advantage. Help your own, that's what I say.'

Unspoken words bank up in Madeleine's mouth. She feels them shrivel to the size of shelled peas. They are being pulled on a thin cord through her throat, down into her stomach. She loses touch with her surroundings and concentrates instead on what is happening to those words. The cord looks like a long, thin rope. It breaks into knotted strands that resemble hauled-in fishing nets. She waits for the pain to begin.

Once the children are asleep, she says her goodnights. In the darkened bedroom she imagines herself lying at the bottom of a lift shaft. The lift is descending, but she cannot move. She cannot call out or even look about her for some means of escape.

Cables dangle menacingly. Her bones have dissolved into a thick mass of jelly, and every muscle in her body is held firmly to the ground by an all-consuming paralysis. Only her eyes are free to move about, darting this way and that in panic, silent witnesses to her hovering fate.

Next morning she is vapour-thin, insubstantial, worried that her feet might press too hard upon the earth. She can feel herself shrinking. She becomes a tiny goldfish, staring out from her glass bowl at a distorted world. Around and around she swims, pausing momentarily at the count of ten to look again.

In the car on the way back to the hospital, she sits with her bag clutched on her lap and stares straight ahead. John visibly relaxes when at last they arrive.

....

That first time John took me to meet his parents, he forgot to mention it was his mother's birthday. He held on to my hand and told me not to worry. His mother wouldn't mind that I didn't have a present, he said; she wasn't the sort to bother about such things. I had conjured up an image of a plump, motherly type with a ready laugh and an easy-going attitude, but the woman who opened the door was thin and tiny and tight-lipped and wore a hairnet that reached halfway down her forehead. I doubted if she'd ever laughed in her life. Mr Roberts' welcoming shout echoed in the space above her head. His face creased in a smile that began near his chin and ended somewhere above his bushy eyebrows. Pumping my hand energetically, he launched into a running commentary about hot weather and flies as we three traipsed down the hall behind him.

On the dresser in the dining room I could see a pot of jam and a jug of whipped cream, set alongside a plate heaped high with scones and partly covered by a crisp, linen tea-towel. I would later learn the jam was strawberry, Mr Roberts' favourite.

He busied himself handing out glasses of sherry, which we three sipped, standing up, while Mrs Roberts brought steaming plates of food to the table — chicken, baked potatoes and pumpkin, sweet potato and peas, and, Mr Roberts confided, her famous creamy onion sauce.

When the meal was over John went to his room and brought out a large cardboard box. He made a great show of handing the box to his mother, helping her open the flaps and removing two round Pyrex bowls. He set the bowls on the table, one on top of the other, then slipped a hollow black plastic cylinder down through the top, connecting the two. A matching black lid completed the arrangement. I'd never seen a coffee percolator like it before.

John produced a flat metal shape with a wooden handle, not unlike a frying pan, designed to protect the bowls from direct heat. Delving deeper into the box, he drew forth a packet of ground coffee beans and handed it to his mother with a knowing wink.

We stood around the stove waiting for the miracle to happen. Somehow, the water in the bottom bowl would rise through the hollow section of the black plastic cylinder, connect with the six spoonfuls of ground beans and, when the liquid finished dripping into the top bowl, the coffee was ready. It was a wondrous thing to watch, and the coffee smelt good.

John filled the cups and Mr Roberts brought the scones, the jam and the whipped cream to the table. Filling my mouth with a piece of scone smeared with jam and cream, I saw that John had poured coffee into three cups, not four. Right then the kettle boiled. Mrs Roberts went into the kitchen, returning moments later with a teapot in her hand.

Perplexed, I could hardly wait to swallow.

'You're not going to try the coffee, Mrs Roberts?' I asked.

'No, I only ever drink tea, and I'm fussy about it too. Few people know how to make a really nice cup of tea.'

From a drawer in the dresser, Mr Roberts took out a pipe and a packet of tobacco. He pushed back his chair and began filling the pipe. Mrs Roberts jumped up like a bullet shot out of a gun and ran to a cupboard near the back door. Collecting a pile of newspapers, she unfolded them on the floor, making a mat at Mr Roberts' feet.

'Now, watch what you're doing, William,' she warned. 'It's bad enough having to clean up after the dog without you making a mess too.'

Afterwards, as we sat in John's car, he answered my questions with a shrug of his shoulders.

'I told you before, Mum doesn't worry about stuff like that . . .'

I was indignant.

'She worries about cooking a good meal and keeping the house clean. What makes you think she wouldn't be upset when her only son buys himself an expensive gift and calls it her birthday present?'

He patted my knee.

'I know it may look odd, but honestly, what I did made her happy. I know it did.'

There were numerous incidents that made me wonder if John and I would ever speak the same language. Once I asked him how much board he paid.

'I give Mum five pounds every week,' he replied. He failed to add, as I later found out, that when he did hand over that five-pound note, his mother handed back one pound change and often two. She also kept the drawers of his wardrobe stocked with new underwear and pyjamas and made sure he never ran short of after-shave, toothpaste or deodorant.

I'd been amused when John told me about the feud that raged between his mother and the next-door neighbours, an elderly man and his grown-up son. The two houses had only one main water pipe, with connections branching off to each house. One day when the son spoke rudely to Iris she wreaked her revenge by turning on every tap in her house, so that not even a trickle of water came through any of the taps next door.

I struggled to keep from laughing.

'How long did she keep it up?'

'It's been three days so far.'

'What? You mean she's wasting all that water?'

I was beginning to see Iris in a new light.

My relationship with John was an on-and-off affair. During the next four years we fought often. After yet another blazing row, our arms thrown up in frustration, we'd stamp off, refusing to answer the phone for weeks or even months at a time.

Then something would happen — we'd meet by chance in the street, or perhaps one of us would decide that just this once it was OK to eat humble pie and call around or write a letter. Bitterness and hurt, softened by the growing habit of familiarity, became part of a shared history that developed a strength of its own, creating a refuge from loneliness, a buffer against other kinds of disappointment. In touch once again, we'd make plans to go out for dinner or to a drive-in, or maybe spend a day at the beach.

John was twenty-six when we got married; I was twenty-three. In those early years, when we were saving our pennies and trying to work out where we could afford to buy a house, our intentions were in harmony. We decorated our rented flat, thrilled to think that it was our first home. It took a while for the cracks to appear, and even longer to accept that they couldn't be patched with dismissive excuses, and that marriage wasn't guaranteed to prevent them from getting worse.

Soft snores, an occasional cough, a woman turning over in a creaky bed – these are the sounds filling the shadowy darkness of the women's ward tonight. Unable to sleep, Madeleine slips out of bed, throws on her dressing gown and heads for the toilet. The light is on. Over near the washbasins a woman is tearing up a sheet. She's dressed only in a flowery cotton nightdress and brown leather boots, but she doesn't seem to notice the cold. She rips sections of material lengthwise from the edge, beginning each new tear with her teeth. A pile of knotted strips lies at her feet.

Madeleine enters one of the toilet cubicles and crouches over the seat to pee. What is the woman intending to do? Maybe she's had bad news? Is she a voluntary patient? Have they forced her into this ward at the last moment? Was she maybe expecting to go home? Oh, why can't I remember her name?

Finished in the toilet, Madeleine crosses the room to wash her hands. She chooses the basin right next to where the woman is standing.

'Audrey, isn't it? What are you doing?'

The woman doesn't even look up.

Madeleine rinses her hands and turns off the tap. She tries to catch the woman's eye.

'Are you OK?'

There is no reply, only a series of ripping sounds.

The night staff are playing cards. Nurse Stanley has his back to Madeleine. She taps gently on the glass panel. He twists around in his swivel chair. Waving her arms about, she mouths the word *HELP* a number of times.

He leans back to say something to the other two. They

laugh as though he's told them the punch line to a joke. Turning his attention to Madeleine, he holds his arm in the air so she can see his watch. He drums his right index finger on the dial, then spreads that hand wide, placing it alongside his left thumb. She already knows the ward is opened at 6 a.m. Can't he understand this is an emergency?

She does not wait to see him wave goodbye with bent-over fingers, nor does she hear the laughter that follows. Nurse Stanley picks up his cards and the game continues.

The woman is shaking so badly now that her nightdress vibrates like a switched-on electrical appliance. Her feet are constantly on the move, caught up in a compulsive jig.

Drawing nearer, taking small steps, Madeleine reaches out, placing her hands on the woman's shoulders.

'Look, I want to help you. Won't you just talk to me?'

An anguished cry escapes from the woman's lips. She pushes Madeleine away.

'Please, please,' Madeleine begs, her heart beginning to thump in a crazy rhythm, like a rabbit in a sack. The woman resumes tying the last few knots.

This time Madeleine hits the flat of her palm against the glass. Nurse Stanley is not impressed. He raises a thumb above his head and dismisses her with an 'up yours' gesture. The other two nurses keep their heads lowered, pretending to be absorbed in the cards, but their mouths twitch as if they could burst out laughing at any moment.

Madeleine stands there dumbfounded.

The woman has found a chair. She positions it beneath a shower head, then pulls herself up, carrying the knotted rope of strips behind her. She ties one end to the shower head, checks the knot is secure, then tosses the rolled-up excess over the partition wall.

In the next stall she takes her time, twisting the material around the shower head a few times, pulling on the slack, testing each knot in turn, before slipping the prepared noose over her head.

'Please, oh, please, don't do this!'

Madeleine is crying. She leans close to the chair and grabs two concertinaed handfuls of flowered nightdress. The woman lashes out blindly. Madeleine hangs on, trying not to think about the bruise that must be forming on her leg. The woman moans incoherently, pulls the nightdress high above her knees and hits out with her heavy boots.

Madeleine staggers back.

The woman seizes this opportunity to kick the chair away. It topples sideways, one of its legs catching on the sloping tiles near the drain-hole. In slow motion it falls, filling the gap between Madeleine and the woman, who is now dangling awkwardly. A few drops of water drip onto the woman's shoulders. Her hands flail about, and she manages to push herself away from the taps. Her weight drags on the rope. A metallic grunt indicates the lead pipe is straining. It might yet pull away from the wall.

Transfixed with horror, Madeleine grabs at the wall, feeling faint but determined to stay with the woman. It seems important somehow. Liquid brown matter pours in a sudden burst from beneath the woman's nightdress. There is a dreadful smell. Anger uncoils in Madeleine's belly. It rises swiftly, shooting up her spine, across her shoulders, along her arms. For one vivid instant she knows she is mad.

Galvanised, she grabs the chair with both hands and swings it high above her head. Her fingers throb. They remind her of sausages cooking under the griller, about to split their skins. She is so hot, so feverish, that globules of sweat form on her upper lip. Maybe her flesh is on fire? She pushes against the toilet door with her backside, holding it open for as long as it takes to lower the chair and pass through. The thoughts in her head are like Jean's painting, whorls of colour that dance and twirl, leading her on. Her mouth is twisted, her face a grotesque mask.

Some of the other patients have woken in fright. They are sitting up in bed, staring in panic. What's going on?

The sound of shattering glass goes on and on.

John and Lindy meet at the hospital gates. He's still in his overalls.

'I'm so glad you were able to come,' he says, opening her car door.

'Look, if it's bad news, John, I'd rather you had someone with you.'

Dr Kemble ushers them into his office. He picks up a chair from the corridor, carries it inside and sets it down next to the other one in front of his desk.

'I came as soon as I could,' John begins.

'Has Madeleine done something stupid?' Lindy asks.

'I don't know about stupid, but she has done some damage. I don't think she was attempting suicide, if that's what you mean. She threw a chair through a window.'

John is about to speak. Lindy rises from her chair.

Dr Kemble stops them with a raised hand.

'Let me tell you what happened.'

He waits until they sit back in their chairs.

'It seems Madeleine was annoyed that none of the night staff would come when she called, so she got hold of a chair and threw it through the glass panel at the end of the ward.

Nurse Stanley had to be treated for cuts to his head and face. He's all right, fortunately, but it's a serious matter.'

John frowns.

'Are you sure it was her?'

'Oh yes, no question about that.'

Lindy returns Dr Kemble's smile with a suspicious stare.

'We're talking here about someone who has no history of violence. We know Madeleine . . .' She points towards John, then back to herself. 'You don't. She wouldn't hurt a fly.'

Lindy strums her fingers on the top of the desk. Her bangles make a grating sound.

'If, and I mean if, Madeleine did do this,' she turns her head to look intently at John, 'I'd want to know what it was that upset her. She's just not the violent type.'

'I agree with you Mrs . . . uh, I'm sorry, I've forgotten your name.'

She waves her hand impatiently.

'You can call me Lindy like everyone else.'

'Well, Lindy, I agree with you. That's why we will not be taking any further action, nor am I planning to note this inci-dent in Madeleine's file, but she has been heavily sedated for her own protection. She will need a few days rest in order to put this out of her mind, to make a fresh start.'

John is bewildered. He shakes his head. Could Madeleine be getting worse?

'Where is she now?' he asks.

'She's back in the room she was in when we admitted her. Under close supervision. You can see her if you like, not that she'll be awake . . .'

John is still shaking his head.

'I thought things were picking up.'

'I'm sure she is better. This is probably a minor setback. She may be getting sick of this place. It might mean she's missing you and the children. That's understandable, isn't it?'

John nods. He is relieved by Dr Kemble's words. 'Thank you for all you're doing, Doctor.'

The two men stand up. John stretches across the desk to shake the doctor's hand. Dr Kemble accompanies them to the door.

'Give it a few days,' he adds as John and Lindy step into the corridor. 'A good sleep is often the best cure.'

They walk along the path. Lindy stops for a moment and reaches into her handbag for her sunglasses.

'I have to tell you, John, I'm beginning to dislike that man. In fact, I wouldn't trust him as far as I could throw him.'

'Oh, I think he's OK. He did say he was going to let the matter drop. That's decent of him, don't you think?'

'Like I said, I don't trust him. He's got shifty eyes.'

....

It is 8 a.m. A nurse comes into the room, lifts the sleeping patient's wrist, takes a pulse reading, then lets the wrist drop back onto the blanket. She reaches for the instruction sheet on the bedside table.

Mrs Roberts is to be given only light medication
Tuesday evening and encouraged to get out of bed for
short periods throughout Wednesday. A close watch is
to be kept on her, noting any untoward symptoms.

The nurse reads Dr Kemble's instructions through once again. Skimming the medication dosage list, she reads the last entry.

5 a.m. Pt had a good night, though there were one or two periods when she moaned and seemed about to wake up.

Nurse Quigley

The nurse makes a note of the pulse reading and initials the appropriate column. She puts the instruction sheet back on the bedside table and turns her attention to the patient. Positioning herself alongside the bed, she gives Madeleine's shoulders a firm shake.

'Atta girl, pull yourself out of it. If you don't, who knows, you might sleep your life away.'

The nurse wipes a damp, cold face-cloth across Madeleine's forehead, under her chin, along each bare arm. Making an effort to keep her eyes open, Madeleine lifts her head and looks about her. The room spins. She sinks back onto the pillow.

'What, what am I doing here?'

Her eyes focus on the plastic bag hanging from a metal stand alongside the bed.

'What's wrong with me?'

The nurse chuckles.

'That's nothing to worry about. You've been in a deep sleep for a few days. We had to feed you intravenously.'

'Why? What happened?'

'You'll have to ask Dr Kemble for the gory details.' The nurse smiles. 'I'm afraid I don't have any answers. I've been looking after you on the day shift since Monday. I'm Nurse Prosser, by the way.'

'So what day is it today?'

'Wednesday.'

'How long have I been . . . been in this heavy sleep?'

Nurse Prosser consults the instruction sheet.

'Since the early hours of Sunday morning.'

Nurse Prosser unrolls the bandage from Madeleine's wrist, removes the needle protruding from the end of the plastic tube, drops it into the kidney bowel and wheels the metal stand into a corner.

Madeleine stares at the ceiling and tries to remember what could have happened in the early hours of Sunday morning. It takes her a moment or two to realise Nurse Prosser is speaking again.

'Would you like some tea and toast? I could get it while you're getting dressed.'

She turns to a pile of clothing, neatly folded on the end of the bed. 'I had to go through your things. What about wearing these today?'

She holds up a pair of jeans and a dark blue cardigan.

Madeleine pulls herself up on her elbows, fighting the giddiness. 'Yes, fine. What did you say your name was?'

'Prosser. Nurse Prosser.'

'Are you new?'

'Goodness, does it show that much? I've been a nurse for several years, but I've never worked in a psychiatric centre before.'

Madeleine answers with the barest hint of a smile.

'It does show, but not for the reason you think.'

Madeleine is grateful she's been left alone. She eases herself out of bed. Her legs are weak and shaky. There's a faint, unpleasant odour. If only she could have a shower. Oh God, the shower. She remembers a flowered nightdress, heavy boots, an upturned chair, the woman who hanged herself.

Dropping to her knees, Madeleine presses her face against the bedclothes to muffle her sobs.

Each tiny detail slots into place. The memory has a dream-like quality, vivid, shocking, but positioned a long way off. She cannot recapture what she felt then, cannot slip on her feelings like a glove. She has a sense of something lost, something stolen from her. Hesitantly, she walks around the room. The dizziness has lessened. She is trembling, and she cannot stop. Leaning against the wall for support, she makes a decision. She has to get out of this place.

....

Once, not long ago – last week, last month, or was it years ago? – a kind-hearted nurse comes to work at one of these psychiatric hospitals. Appalled, even alarmed, at what she sees, she allows sympathy to creep into her eyeballs. The patients know immediately. They are alert to the smallest difference. When they smile, she smiles back; when they cry, her face shows signs of compassion. Aha. Tentative at first, they tell her their stories, over and over again. The nurse is patient. She listens and gives what comfort she can, privately thinking this is what she is here for.

At the end of some shifts she returns home feeling sad and confused. Tears slide unnoticed down her face, nestling in the outer corners of her lips.

At this stage empathy and sympathy are hopelessly entwined. They track a vein in the good-hearted nurse's arm, puncture a tiny hole on the inside of her elbow, and slip unnoticed into her bloodstream.

Shock shows on the faces of other staff when they notice her fingers stroke a patient's face. Soon they are muttering behind their hands to each other when she walks by. Have you noticed how she talks to them? *As though they were friends.*

Too late, the good-hearted nurse realises she has become

involved. She cares what happens to the patients. Now that is a dangerous thing.

Before long the good-hearted nurse is the butt of jokes. She is labelled a 'pushover', told she's gone soft in the head. Doctors openly chastise her, insisting she develop a 'more professional approach'. Her attempts to explain her methods are met by a solid wall of disapproval.

The good-hearted nurse resigns. She scurries away that last day, relief and anger snapping at her heels. What should she have done? What could she have done? She feels ashamed. What will happen to the patients? Does anyone care? What should she have done? What could she have done?

She can't sleep. She tosses and turns night after night. She wonders how Betty is getting on. Did her sister visit, as she promised? Did George get to make that phone call? And what about Ruth and Sam? Does anyone care? She thumps the pillow in frustration. Something should be done, something really ought to be done, but what?

Fortunately, as time passes, the good-hearted nurse finds another job. She's busy, she makes plans, she's even sleeping better. Like dreams, her concerns about Betty and George and Ruth and Sam fade away, drifting down corridors, along passageways, until they come to rest in a remote corner of her mind.

NURSING NOTES WARD 5

Specify Case History or Nursing Notes

V.C.N. Blight, Government Printer

SURNAME	FIRST NAMES	AGE	SEX	WARD
ROBERTS	MADELEINE MR719056		F	5

Sep 12 – 5.30 p.m.
Pt has been up since 8.30 a.m. Appears a little confused
but has been pleasant and co-operative all day.
> Nurse Prosser

Sep 12 – 11 p.m.
Hd visited this evening. Asked him, as instructed, not to
confuse pt with questions. Pt dozed off several times.
Appears calm overall.
> Nurse Quigley

Sep 13 – 7 a.m.
Pt had a restful night.
> Nurse Quigley

Sep 13 – 3 p.m.
Pt seems much brighter today. Has eaten breakfast but
hardly touched lunch. Shows no sign of distress.
> Nurse Prosser

Nov 12 – 11.30 p.m.
Pt calm. Appears to have no recall of recent events.
> Nurse Quigley

Sep 14 – 7 a.m.
Pt had a peaceful night.
> Nurse Quigley

Sep 14 – 3 p.m.
Pt presents as calm and in good spirits. Suggest
Dr Kemble might want to see her. She appears ready to be
returned to the ward.
> Nurse Prosser

RYDALMERE PSYCHIATRIC CENTRE

MEMO

TO: Nurse Quigley, Ward 5   **DATE**: 18th September

FROM: Dr Kemble

REFERENCE: Madeleine Roberts – Patient No. MR719056

MFH 627 – B   V.C.N. Blight, Government Printer

I am planning to discharge pt in the near future but wish to begin a
programme of –

1.   Anatensol Enanthate intra-muscular injection fortnightly to
        be administered at Ward 5. Regular fortnightly appointment
        between pt and staff.

2.   Cogentin 2 mg daily.

Could you please set up a SPECIAL MEDICATION SHEET to be kept
on hand and updated after each fortnightly appointment.

I will advise pt that failing to keep appointments will result in
prompt involuntary admission to Rydalmere.

Please emphasise this point yourself in conversation with pt.

First injection to be administered 19th September.

Possible discharge date – 26th September.

. . . .
Eleanor Brown signing
on behalf of Dr Kemble

DISCHARGE SUMMARY

DATE: 26th September

AGE:

NAME: ROBERTS, M

RECORD NO: MR719056

ADMITTED:

DISCHARGED: 26th September

REFERRED BY: Liverpool Hospital

Final diagnosis: Paranoid schizophrenia – Relapse

This patient has a long history of emotional disturbance, variously described as neurotic depression, character neurosis, and ruminative obsessive neurosis. However, since before this last admission she has been consistently diagnosed as a schizophrenic (see earlier notes in file on proverb interpretation) and has received E.C.T. and extensive drug treatment.

She has been admitted previously to Parramatta Psychiatric Centre. When admitted to this hospital her state of mind was described by nursing staff as verbose and tangential. She did not then show signs of psychosis and it was felt that a complete decompensation could be prevented by active drug treatment.

She was treated with Largactil 100 mg four times a day which was later replaced by Stelazine 5 mg twice daily. She has improved considerably and there has been no sign of psychosis.

Intramuscular treatment, Anatensol 12.5 mg, is to be administered fortnightly plus Cogentin 2 mg daily for side-effects. The patient will present herself to Ward 5 for this treatment. A letter notifying her GP has been forwarded as per this discharge date.

TREATMENT ON DISCHARGE: Anatensol Enanthate 12.5 mg
fortnightly
Cogentin 2 mg daily.

FUTURE MANAGEMENT: Ward 5 reports and medication sheet update.

SUMMARIES TO: Medical Records and Dr Gardiner (GP)

Signature . . . .
Eleanor Brown signing on behalf of
Dr Kemble

Patient's name: Madeleine Roberts

TREATMENT CHART

Anatensol 12.5 mgm fortnightly

Long acting Fluphenazine Enanthate (intramuscular)

PLEASE DO NOT REMOVE THIS SHEET – STAFF NEED A RECORD FOR THESE INJECTIONS.

DATE	DOSE	ANTI-PARKINSON AGENT	DOCTOR'S SIGNATURE
19/9	12.5 mgm	Anatensol Administered to hip	

PART 3

Counting the Rivers

Counting
the Rivers

There are sixty-five terry-towelling nappies on the shelf in Christopher's bedroom and eight on the line. Seventy-three? She bought three dozen when Michael was born and another three dozen for Christopher. The total should be seventy-two, not seventy-three.

She moves on to the chest of drawers in Michael's room. She counts his socks several times. The blue ones she bought him last Christmas are missing. She remembers them distinctly. They have Donald Duck faces on both sides of the top edge.

She rummages among his toys, continuing her search. What is it about socks? Could there be some yet-undiscovered animal hiding out in suburbia, forced to live on a strict diet of socks? Damn you, socks, wherever you are. And damn you, number seventy-three. Oh dear, what if she's pinched another child's nappy?

Out in the back yard she counts again. Eight snowy white nappies blowing in the breeze. If one white nappy should accidentally fall she'd be . . . she'd be . . . well, she'd be off the hook. They look worn, hardly any nap left on any of them. Just as well Christopher is almost potty trained.

She leans out from the line to check on the children. Crouched over his cars, Michael is talking to himself and fending off Christopher's attempts to pick up a car. He catches her eye.

'Make him go away, Mum. He doesn't know how to play proply.'

'He wants to do what you're doing, love. You could teach him how to play.'

Michael warms to the idea. His face lights up.

'I will if he's got his own cars.'

'Michael, Michael, what a little con-man you are!'

Madeleine sneaks up behind Christopher, wrapping her arms around his waist, lifting him high into the air. He squeals with delight. Holding him on her hip, she unpegs a dry towel, spreads it out on the grass and lies Christopher down on his back. She blows raspberries on his belly and rubs her face against his delicious flesh. He giggles and chortles, unaware he's being distracted. She looks around for a few of his toys and sets them down near him. No, he doesn't like the look of those. He wants to drag his tractor around.

John's socks hang in a row. The black pair would be better on the end; she moves them round. Her once-white under-wear is soaking in a small bucket. She lifts a bra from the soapy water and wrings it firmly. Just look at it – she doesn't dare use bleach again. Holy underwear? She falters for a moment, then reaches across for more pegs. What was it her mother used to say? 'A pin-up girl is any woman who needs safety pins to keep herself modest.' Madeleine grew up with a dread about pinning anything. She and Lizzie even devised a game they called *what would you do if*.

What would you do if . . . your skirt caught on a branch while you were climbing a tree and you hung there with those tattered, pinned panties exposed for all to see?

What would you do if . . . you were stuck in the bathroom of the Ritz Hotel honeymoon suite, struggling with the rusty safety pin on your bra, while your brand new husband paced up and down outside, breathless with anticipation?

Madeleine's idea of luxury would be a dozen pairs of swish knickers with good elastic and a range of comfy-fitting bras in different colours – maybe even matching sets?

Hurriedly she obscures the sight of her underwear by moving John's overalls. Bending low, she winds up the handle on the Hills Hoist.

On the top step she pauses, taking in the yard with a sweeping glance. John is up the back tinkering with the mower and Michael is near by, moving his cars towards the tea-tree, one by one. She smiles at the sight of Christopher. He is spinning the wheels of his upturned tractor and talking to himself. To her right is a large cement slab and two straight paths that run along the side of the house towards the front gate. John did the cement work before Michael was born, but they still can't afford a garage. At night, when their old VW is parked there, it looks like a toy that's been left out in the rain.

A paling fence, divided into sections by timber posts, borders the yard on all three sides. There are seven posts down each side, eight across the back and eighteen palings in each section. That's a total of three hundred and forty-two palings. She's walked along the fence numerous times in the past two weeks to check her calculations. Did the builders order the same number for each yard, or did they know to the very last paling how many they needed?

Twenty-five houses dominate the view. She can only see the front guttering on the twenty-fifth house because it's on a corner. Fibro houses. Pastel-painted houses. Red-roofed houses. Oxo-cube houses. She'd need a ladder to see all the others in the streets further over.

Just five years ago, there'd only been this one street of half-finished structures, and not a tree or a bush anywhere in sight. High Hope Homes must have made a fortune. Now they have estates all over the place.

She and John had come rushing out one Saturday morning in answer to a big ad in the *Sydney Morning Herald*. It was like a dream come true. Four hundred and eighty pounds deposit and a twenty-five-year mortgage plan with the Rural Bank. Most other banks stipulated a deposit of at least two thousand pounds. When decimal currency came in, the monthly payment was changed from nineteen pounds and eight shillings to thirty-eight dollars and eighty cents.

'Macarthur' is still the second-cheapest of the seven designs on offer, and the best they could afford.

Next door has a back veranda complete with wrought-iron railing and enough room for an outdoor table and chairs, but 'Macarthur' comes with a narrow, raised walkway stretching part way across the width of the house, a toilet positioned at one end, a set of steps at the other. There is no sewerage, but a tar-sprayed pan is provided by the council and replaced once a week by the sani-men who come in the dead of night and only sometimes slop the contents onto the floor. At Christmas time residents show their gratitude by leaving generous tips or a few bottles of beer. The kitchen entrance and the laundry are in the middle of the walkway, and the space is so narrow there's not even enough room to sit on a chair. Madeleine worries that someone will fall off the edge.

It had rained heavily the week before they moved in. John threw down a few lengths of timber so she could get to the clothes-line. Next morning, she put on John's gumboots and set off down the steps. The planks gave way beneath her weight, disappearing into the wet ooze with faint sucking sounds. She began to sink. John came running in answer to her shout, doubling over with laughter at the sight of her. She was down past her knees before he pulled her free. The gumboots had filled with mud, and she couldn't move, but she'd hung on to the washing basket with grim-faced determination. Later she would boast that not one speck of mud had got onto the clothes. They never did see the planks again.

She thinks the Hills Hoist looks ridiculous, sticking out like a sore toe, like all the sore toes in all the other back yards.

Christopher's cry makes her drop the basket. He has hurt his finger. She runs down the steps and scoops him up in her arms. He stops crying immediately.

'Come on Michael, love,' she calls. 'John, it's time for lunch.'

Patient's name: Madeleine Roberts

TREATMENT CHART

Anatensol 12.5 mgm fortnightly

Long acting Fluphenazine Enanthate (intramuscular)

PLEASE DO NOT REMOVE THIS SHEET – STAFF NEED A RECORD FOR THESE INJECTIONS.

DATE	DOSE	ANTI-PARKINSON AGENT	DOCTOR'S SIGNATURE
19/9	12.5 mgm	Anatensol Administered to hip	
3/10	12.5 mgm	Anatensol Administered to hip	
17/10	12.5 mgm	Anatensol Administered to hip	
31/10	12.5 mgm	Anatensol Administered to hip	

The swordfish emerges from the narrow opening between two rocks, then passes in front of the oyster shell, turning sharply to continue in a figure of eight. A silvery gleam flashes through the greenery and behind the line of bubbles that rises from the fake pearl, disappearing with a final tail-flick into the grotto that John finished making only last week.

Madeleine is mesmerised. She is convinced the fish is a part of the dilemma swishing around in her brain. There's something here that she needs to understand.

She'd like to write a description of the fish, but her vision blurs each time she attempts even a few words. She has the same problem with telephone books, but has finally worked out a system. If she holds her finger over a name, like the surname Jones for example, then looks away briefly, she can continue searching for the right initial for a few seconds more before the tightly packed words begin to jump about again.

She's learnt to avoid street directories, and asks John to repeat directions several times. Not that this happens often – she doesn't leave the house much these days – but she did have to take Michael to see a specialist recently about his feet. She was sick and anxious all morning, despite her medication, right up until the moment she walked into the building, and even then she had to ask, because she couldn't read any of the names on the brass plate. In the waiting room Michael crawled onto her lap, wanting her to read him the cartoon story he'd found in a magazine. She made up words to fit each caption, painfully aware of the people in nearby chairs. She thought her voice sounded like an echo. When the doctor called Michael's name, she sprang to her feet so fast she almost toppled the poor kid onto the floor. It's been years since she used her library card, though she used to borrow three and four books a month.

The swordfish appears again. It is coming towards her. At the last moment it makes a left-hand turn and plunges into a nosedive. What if she imagines a blank page inside her head? She won't remember for long, but it's better than nothing.

Mister Swordfish is four inches long and as thin as a dinner plate. Beautiful too, if you like that sort of thing.

· Two brightly coloured fish dart out from the grotto. Madeleine puts her face close to the glass. John bought twelve guppies two weeks ago. She can only see five. Another two are hiding in the weeds, and here come two more females. Madeleine knows they are females because their tails are not vivid like the male guppies'. She spots two more males. She looks away, then counts again.

On the sand, piled high against the glass in the front right-hand corner, she can see something resembling a fragment of prawn shell. Glowering at the swordfish, she yells, 'You bloody murderer!'

Madeleine is reluctant to tell John about her suspicions. If he asks she'll tell him; if he doesn't, she won't.

Next morning breakfast is over early. She is impatient for John to leave. He can't find his car keys anywhere. Madeleine remembers seeing them on his bedside table. By the time he's out the door she's dressed the boys and made the beds. She walks Michael to school. He thinks he's all grown up now. Sister Gertrude waves to her from across the playground. Christopher is in the stroller. He enjoys the fast ride home.

He thumps his hands noisily on the tray of his highchair.

He can hardly wait. Madeleine selects a banana from the bowl on the table, peels it, then cuts it into three pieces with a knife. Next, she takes an arrowroot biscuit from the tin on the shelf and breaks it into four.

Christopher studies the array of food on his tray. Ignoring the banana, he bangs his fist down on a square of biscuit, then shoves the scattered bits into his mouth. Crumbs get mixed in with the dribble running down his chin. There are more crumbs gathering in the corners of the tray. He uses the flat of his hand to shove more biscuit into his mouth. His mouth is so full his lips won't close. He coughs and splutters and delights in the spraying effect. He is totally absorbed.

So is Madeleine. She's on her knees, mouth open, eyes fixed on another corpse. It's a female guppy this time. Ten little guppy lives dangling on a thread. That bloody fish, he's got to go.

She finds the gadget she's after in John's box of aquarium supplies. It has a handle at the end of a metal ring attached to a length of sock-type material. She lowers the pointed end into the water. Madeleine hasn't ever seen the tank from above the water line. There are so many ripples and bubbles, it's a completely new perspective. The socky thing is in there, but it isn't where she thinks it is, and everything seems larger, including the fish.

The swordfish is frantic. Maybe it knows she's after him? He's cagey too. Just when she thinks she's in the right spot, he slips out of reach. Ahh, got something. She inspects her catch. Damn, it's one of the angel fish. She eases it back into the water and turns the handle slightly, shaking the fish free. Her next haul is another angel fish and two guppies. Safely back in the water, the guppies jump about like mobile neon lights.

She moves her arm to a more comfortable position and catches a flickering glimpse of silver further down. What luck. Stupid fish. You swam right into it.

In the bathroom Madeleine upends the sock over the toilet.

'See how you cope with the sewer, you evil creature,' she shouts as the swordfish drops into the bowl.

A running argument starts up in her head.

Christopher has banana in his hair. She steps in another bit when she wipes the mess off the tray. He tries to help by rubbing the front of his shirt. It's her fish tank too. She runs tepid water into the bath, undresses Christopher and helps him climb over the edge. She passes him a collection of plastic containers one at a time, and makes sure the shampoo and soap are out of his reach. Why does John act as though everything belongs to him?

She squirts washing-up liquid onto the highchair seat and scrubs vigorously. It's the same with those orchids. She turns the chair on its side, bending over to wipe each leg in turn. Who needs a hundred-odd specimens of those bloody things anyway?

Christopher is wrapped in a towel. She carries him out to the kitchen table. He squirms in her arms. The kids haven't even got a sandpit, and John's talking about an orchid house.

She pats Christopher dry and pulls the singlet over his head. Suddenly she feels awful. She has an urge to shit, and feels a damp slipperiness on the inside of her thighs. She wants to run away. She imagines her limbs flying out from her body, like propellers gone haywire. How far would she have to run before she dropped down dead? Her dreams are all about running—no, not running, but a certain kind of paralysis that takes hold the minute she readies herself to sprint.

Funny, really; it's not as if she has ever been an athlete. The only time she ever ran around with any speed was when she played basketball, and that was long before she got married. She'd been playing in a senior competition the year she met John. Slowly she counts to ten. Running is out of the question. Tell me something else I *can* do.

Christopher twists to one side, struggling to get on his knees and crawl out of her grasp. She dangles a shoe above his head. He waves his arms about. She lets him pull the shoe towards his chest, then lifts it high again. The game makes him laugh and keeps him on his back long enough for her to finish getting him dressed.

Her movements are robotic, automatic, repetitive. She mops the kitchen floor. The curtains need washing too. She's been putting it off for weeks. Why doesn't John notice how many things they need? The curtain rings are fiddly. It takes ages to unhook the first one; three more to go. OK, so he earns the odd tip from a happy customer. Does that make it his money? She steps down from the chair, bundles up the curtains and takes them out to the laundry. Christopher is close behind. What opportunity has she got to earn money or tips anyhow? The kitchen door hasn't closed properly. Christopher pulls it open and stumbles in his haste. She picks him up roughly and shudders with the urge to throw him down onto the grass. Shocked, clutching him tightly, she rushes inside, removing them both from danger.

She lets him play with two of Michael's cars. He walks around the kitchen, one in each hand, trying them on for size. She wants to tell him she's sorry, but he's too little to understand. She's an adult and she doesn't understand either. What would make her do such a thing?

On the way out the door to collect Michael, she looks across at the fish tank. She remembers how the swordfish looked before it fell into the toilet bowl, like a tiddler you throw back in the sea because it's too small to eat. Her lips tighten. She hasn't changed her mind. He deserved it.

During the night she gets up to pee. John has left the fish-tank light on. She perches on the edge of the lounge and counts. Five, six, seven, eight, nine. The latest corpse is in the usual place on the sand.

Hurriedly she unlocks the back door, her fingers fumbling with the key. Laughter bubbles up. She can't stop it — she has to get outside.

Nine neon bodies hanging on a thread,
if one little swordfish should accidentally fall,
then there's no bloody difference, no
diff-er-ence at all.

Patient's name: Madeleine Roberts

TREATMENT CHART

Anatensol 12.5 mgm fortnightly
Long acting Fluphenazine Enanthate (intramuscular)

PLEASE DO NOT REMOVE THIS SHEET – STAFF NEED A RECORD FOR THESE INJECTIONS.

DATE	DOSE	ANTI-PARKINSON AGENT	DOCTOR'S SIGNATURE
19/9	12.5 mgm	Anatensol Administered to hip	
3/10	12.5 mgm	Anatensol Administered to hip	
17/10	12.5 mgm	Anatensol Administered to hip	
31/10	12.5 mgm	Anatensol Administered to hip	
14/11	12.5 mgm	Anatensol Administered to hip	
28/11	12.5 mgm	Anatensol Administered to hip	
12/12	12.5 mgm	Anatensol Administered to hip	
12/12		Prescription for Cogentin issued	

Cora Brent is at screaming point. Nothing has gone right for months. How many times has she asked Carl to ring the solicitor, to find out where they stand? Every time she asks him about it, he just shrugs his shoulders and mumbles some feeble excuse.

She'll have to see the estate agent again. The forecast is for rain – she told him that last week. How would he like it if his house was built on top of an old river bed? She shakes her fist in the direction of his office.

'Yeah, Mr Glover, how would you like knowing your house could be washed away? You with your mealy-mouthed grin!'

She's so upset she wants to cry, but what good will that do? She'll make a cup of tea. Maybe she should write to the local MP?

Thump thump, diddley dum. Thump thump, diddley dum. Oh, not again. Cora rushes down the hall to her bedroom window and pulls back the curtain. The front door of the house opposite is open, and she can see inside through their screen door. If this keeps up she'll be back in bed with another migraine. That woman. That crazy woman.

Madeleine is dancing. The music makes her feel good. She wants to lose herself in it. She struts a few steps with Michael, holding his hands in hers, moving him in a circle. Christopher lets out a yell of protest. Madeleine lets go one of Michael's hands and gently pulls Christopher forward.

'Take his hand, Michael,' she yells above the sound of Mama Cass. Christopher's laughter is contagious. Michael catches it on the wing, then passes it on. Madeleine's chuckle is quieter, but the boys don't care.

Madeleine doesn't hear Cora shout, but the sound of the hammer banging on the fibro wall startles her. Panicked, she lets go of Christopher and he drops to the floor on his bottom.

He hasn't decided yet whether to laugh or cry. Michael rushes to the door alongside his mother. The music plays on.

Madeleine unclips the screen door. Cora is on the front veranda, brandishing a hammer. What does she want? They've only ever smiled and waved across the street before, but now they glare at each other like enemies.

Cora raises her voice even louder.

'You turn that bloody noise down now or I'm gonna smash this hammer right through every friggin' record you own. Do you hear me?'

Madeleine's hand rests on Michael's shoulder, keeping him pinned close to her side. There are no words clamouring in her head. She can't think of a single one.

Cora feels the first twinges of pain. There are whirling spots in front of her eyes. She must get to bed. Leaning forward, taking care to keep her head perfectly still, she directs her attention to Michael. He can't understand what she's saying.

'Poor, poor liddle boy. Fanshy having to live with a mad muvver. Mad Madeleine, mad, mad Madeleine.'

She continues to mutter incoherently. At the gate she turns back and shakes the hammer.

'Yoush been warned, mad Madeleine. I'll get choo. You'll see.'

Madeleine locks the clip on the screen door, then closes the front door.

The record has stopped. She lifts it off the spindle and turns it over, ready to play the other side. Christopher is bouncing up and down, but Michael stands near the door watching his mother as though waiting for a signal.

She smiles at him reassuringly.

'Shall we play it a bit louder this time?'

Patient's name: Madeleine Roberts

TREATMENT CHART

Anatensol 12.5 mgm fortnightly

Long acting Fluphenazine Enanthate (intramuscular)

PLEASE DO NOT REMOVE THIS SHEET – STAFF NEED A RECORD FOR THESE INJECTIONS.

DATE	DOSE	ANTI-PARKINSON AGENT	DOCTOR'S SIGNATURE
19/9	12.5 mgm	Anatensol Administered to hip	
3/10	12.5 mgm	Anatensol Administered to hip	
17/10	12.5 mgm	Anatensol Administered to hip	
31/10	12.5 mgm	Anatensol Administered to hip	
14/11	12.5 mgm	Anatensol Administered to hip	
28/11	12.5 mgm	Anatensol Administered to hip	
12/12	12.5 mgm	Anatensol Administered to hip	
12/12		Prescription for Cogentin issued	
26/12	12.5 mgm	Anatensol Administered to hip	
9/1	12.5 mgm	Anatensol Administered to hip	
23/1	12.5 mgm	Anatensol Administered to hip	
6/2	12.5 mgm	Anatensol Administered to hip	
20/2	12.5 mgm	Anatensol Administered to hip	

Nurse Quigley tosses the used needle into a kidney bowl.

'Dr Kemble wants to see you today. He's in his office. Don't stand there looking like a shop dummy – he'll be wanting to get away for his lunch.'

Dr Kemble looks at Madeleine blankly, and for a moment she wonders if he recognises her.

'Sit down, Madeleine, sit down. Are you finding the injections helpful? No little green men in flying saucers troubling you?'

He laughs. She doesn't.

'My arms and legs twitch a lot.'

He has already noticed the involuntary movements of her elbows and hands, and the weight she's put on.

He makes a note on her file.

'It takes a while for the drugs to get into your system. Don't worry, it will settle down in a few more weeks. I see you've put on some weight . . .'

She's wearing her best pair of jeans. They fit, but the zip was hard to do up this morning. She was eight stone two pounds before she was admitted to Parramatta. She can't be all that fat, surely?

'Are you eating more than usual?'

'No but I drink more. I have a terrible thirst.'

She doesn't mention she's getting through several family-sized bottles of Coca-cola a week. The dryness is worse in the evenings. That's when she takes swigs from the cold bottle in the fridge.

About that thirst. She's in the process of formulating a question, but can't get the words out in time.

'We've had a complaint.'

He strokes the top of his steepled fingers against his chin.

A complaint?

'Out in the big, wide world,' he points the steeple to the world beyond his window, 'we have to do our best to get along with people, to be courteous and considerate . . .'

She keeps her eyes on his hands. What's he leading up to?

'. . . and if outpatients prove themselves a nuisance to society, then it's our responsibility to readmit them . . .'

She hears her voice. She's asked a question. Surprisingly, the words make sense.

'Have I done something wrong, Doctor?'

'I'm going to ask you that question, Madeleine. Have you done something wrong?'

She doesn't hesitate.

'No, I haven't. I'm sorry if I sound rude, but I don't know what you're talking about, really I don't.'

'Isn't that the problem, though? When a person is mentally ill or recovering from breakdown, they may not know how they're coming across. They may not want to know how offensive their behaviour is.'

There is silence in the room. Christopher struggles to get down off her lap. Madeleine removes a bunch of keys from her handbag and dangles them to attract his attention. She puts the keys into his outstretched hand.

Her mind is buzzing. A complaint. What sort of complaint? Who on earth would ring and complain about her? It couldn't be Lindy or John, and she hardly sees anyone else. Besides, who but those two even know her doctor's name? But maybe the person didn't know. Maybe they rang the hospital and mentioned *her* name.

Dr Kemble watches her face carefully.

'I'm going to ask you again, Madeleine. Have you done something wrong?'

He catches the flash of anger.

'Do you need me to ask the question again?'

'No.'

'You've remembered?'

'I remember an incident with a neighbour.'

'Good. Good. We'll say no more then, shall we? You do realise I cannot give you any names or details, but I think a warning is enough, don't you? You're making good progress, Madeleine. Let's keep it that way, eh?'

....

Before she leaves the service-station counter Madeleine checks the change in her hand. She gave him twenty dollars, not ten.

'Keith, you've made a mistake.'

'Not me, love, I don't believe in 'em.'

'The petrol was eight dollars and I gave you twenty.'

'Nah, that's wishful thinking, Madeleine.'

'I tell you I did. I know, 'cos it's all I've got. I have to go to the bank today for the shopping money.'

'Hang around, then. I'll check next time I open the till.'

Cora Brent appears at Madeleine's shoulder.

'Causing trouble again, are we?' she asks with a sneer.

Madeleine speaks through clenched teeth. 'You stay out of this.'

Cora pretends she's offended. 'I'm a customer. I've a perfect right to be here, haven't I, Keith?'

He grins but says nothing. He's staying out of this one.

Just then Lindy appears at the door.

'What's taking so long?' she asks.

Cora's sneer melts. 'Hi, Lindy, how's your mother? On the mend now?'

'Yes, thanks, Cora. You right, Madeleine?'

'Yeah, Keith is going to check the till.'

Cora hands over her money. Keith rings up the amount. The drawer opens. A moment later he reaches across the counter with a ten-dollar note in his hand.

'Sorry, love, must be one of those days.'

Madeleine grabs the money, tosses him an exasperated smile and follows Lindy out to the car.

Christopher and Rodney are huddled together on the back seat. Lindy opens the passenger door.

'Rodney, move over and give Christopher some room.'

'But I'm showing him my truck.'

'That's great, but I still want you to move over a little.'

Lindy waits till he shifts a few tiny inches, then she gets into her seat. Madeleine is turning the key in the ignition. Lindy keeps her voice low.

'What was that all about?'

'Wait till I get outta here and I'll tell you.'

Madeleine checks the rear-vision mirror, then looks back over her shoulder. Cora is coming out of the garage doorway.

'I could kill that woman,' Madeleine mutters.

'Don't let her get to you. It will only make things worse.'

Madeleine moves the gearstick into first.

'She's making my life hell. I think she's watching my every move. Wherever I go, she's under my armpit.'

Lindy chuckles. 'You never know, she might be fond of armpits.'

Madeleine drives out of the garage and along Phillip Avenue.

'It's no joke, Lindy,' she replies impatiently.

Patient's name: Madeleine Roberts

TREATMENT CHART

Anatensol 12.5 mgm fortnightly

Long acting Fluphenazine Enanthate (intramuscular)

PLEASE DO NOT REMOVE THIS SHEET – STAFF NEED A RECORD FOR THESE INJECTIONS.

DATE	DOSE	ANTI-PARKINSON AGENT	DOCTOR'S SIGNATURE
19/9	12.5 mgm	Anatensol Administered to hip	
3/10	12.5 mgm	Anatensol Administered to hip	
17/10	12.5 mgm	Anatensol Administered to hip	
31/10	12.5 mgm	Anatensol Administered to hip	
14/11	12.5 mgm	Anatensol Administered to hip	
28/11	12.5 mgm	Anatensol Administered to hip	
12/12	12.5 mgm	Anatensol Administered to hip	
12/12		Prescription for Cogentin issued	
26/12	12.5 mgm	Anatensol Administered to hip	
9/1	12.5 mgm	Anatensol Administered to hip	
23/1	12.5 mgm	Anatensol Administered to hip	
6/2	12.5 mgm	Anatensol Administered to hip	
20/2	12.5 mgm	Anatensol Administered to hip	

Patient's name: Madeleine Roberts

TREATMENT CHART

Anatensol 12.5 mgm fortnightly

Long acting Fluphenazine Enanthate (intramuscular)

PLEASE DO NOT REMOVE THIS SHEET – STAFF NEED A RECORD FOR THESE INJECTIONS.

DATE	DOSE	ANTI-PARKINSON AGENT	DOCTOR'S SIGNATURE
6/3	12.5 mgm	Anatensol Administered to hip	
20/3	12.5 mgm	Anatensol Administered to hip	
3/4	12.5 mgm	Anatensol Administered to hip	
17/4	12.5 mgm	Anatensol Administered to hip	

John hands Madeleine a mug of tea.

'Is that sweet enough?'

'Yes, fine, thanks.'

He puts his mug on the coffee table and turns to watch the film on the TV.

'Is this bloke the one who killed the girl?'

'I think so – I still can't get the gist of it. Can we turn it off?'

'Ah, come on, it's only just started.'

Annoyed, she puts her mug down hard. A small amount of tea slops over the rim.

'I've been trying to talk to you ever since you got home.'

He keeps his attention on the television set.

'I told you before, you're making a fuss over nothing. So she's in the chemist's shop. So what? She lives in this street, for Christ's sake! Of course, she'll be around.'

'It's not that simple, John. Didn't you hear what I said? It was her who made the complaint. Kemble as much as said so.'

He turns his head slightly towards her.

'I want to watch this, Madeleine. Can't we talk some other time?'

'When? When do we ever talk? I'm trying to tell you something, something that's more important than a bloody film.'

He jumps up, flicks off the TV knob, spins on his heel and points a finger at her chest.

'You're paranoid, you know that? No one can even look at you any more. All I want is a quiet life, like any other man. I work hard, Madeleine. At home I just want a bit of peace and quiet . . .'

He rubs his hands through his hair in a slow swipe either side of his temples.

'Now, is that asking too much?'

The expression on his face is ugly.

'Well, you've got my full attention. Come on, then. Oh no, I get it, I'm gonna get the silent treatment, right?'

If he says one more word . . .

John strides around the room and comes to a halt, leaning one hand on the kitchen door.

'I'm putting up with a lot from you . . .'

She springs out of her chair. Her eyes have a steely glint. Surprised, he steps to one side, dodges her hand and grabs hold of her wrist. She makes a swing at him with her left hand but he grabs that one too.

He shoves her back on the lounge.

'Look at yourself. You're behaving like a child. Now calm down, or I'll have to phone Dr Kemble.'

Next morning he's up early, busy with the electric drill. The frame goes up quickly. He expects to have the whole thing finished by tomorrow night, shelves and all. Then he can buy more orchids.

It's ten o'clock. He comes inside, fills the kettle and lights the front ring on the stove.

'Hey, Madeleine, can you keep Michael in here for a while?'

She's carrying dirty towels out of the bathroom.

'Want a cup of tea?' he asks as she walks past.

'No, thanks.'

He cups her elbow and gently turns her round.

'What's up?'

She looks at the floor, at the wall, then at him.

'I think up is the opposite of down.'

He releases her quickly.

'God, I make a bloody effort and look what you do! Why won't you answer me properly?'

'Because I don't think you're saying anything.'

He takes a step closer and looks her full in the face.

'You'd know, wouldn't you? After all, you're the one who's paranoid. Paranoid schizophrenic. That's what you are.'

Slowly she steps outside. She'll put the towels in the washing machine, add a few spoonfuls of powder, close the lid, and turn on the switch. She will not dwell on those two words, but they won't go away. They are drumbeats in her brain.

paranoid schizophrenic
para-noid-schizo-phren-ic
par-a-noid-schi-zo-phren-ic

John is at the laundry door. She will not look at him. She will not give anything away. Keep your face solemn, eyes down. Act like you don't feel anything. You wouldn't show your fear to a mad dog, would you?

She takes a dishcloth from beneath the sink and begins to wipe the top of the washing machine. She's busy. She can find lots to do.

He is back in the kitchen. She can hear him moving around. He comes out the back door with a mug of tea. At the bottom of the steps he hesitates. He's halfway up the yard before he sees Michael is playing with his tools.

'Put that hammer down! I've told you before, you can hurt yourself. Now get inside, go on.'

Kiama is famous for its blowhole. The Aboriginal word is kia-rama, meaning 'where the sea makes a noise'. And it does.

Throughout the 1950s the blowhole was my father's favourite destination for a Sunday drive, especially during winter, when squally seas would force ocean swells through this natural hole in the rock and the resounding boooom and the height of the spray would draw involuntary gasps from the onlookers.

On those windy Sundays the grassy mound above the rocks was a safe retreat from which I could observe my father's fascination. His mouth, a small slash in an unyielding face, would widen slightly as the boom sounded, but it was more like a grimace than a smile.

It is here at Kiama, all these years later, that I connect with the enormous power he once held over me. He'd been dead nine months before anyone bothered to tell me, and I never did ask where he was buried. No grave could hold the same meaning as the blowhole. It exists for me still as an uncanny metaphor.

My father's lifelong history of constipation weighed heavily on our family. He'd begun taking laxatives of one sort or another before I was born, and for as long as I can remember he purchased bulk supplies of paraffin oil in half-gallon jars from the local chemist. The jars were made of glass and came in two colours, dark brown and dark green. The short neck ended in a large pouring hole. Every night he put the upturned rim against his jutting bottom lip and glugged down a generous mouthful.

Thanks to this daily dose of paraffin, his bowel movements were almost as reliable as the mantelpiece clock. A series of explosive noises from my parents' bedroom warned the rest of the household to stay off the stairs and away from the only toilet, which was in the back yard, around the corner from the kitchen door. Sometimes the warnings were urgent. On these occasions he'd come rushing towards the stairs, left hand clutching his stomach, right hand outstretched ready to grab the banister rail and throw himself over it, landing on both feet with a loud thud.

I used to lie in bed hoping he'd break his neck or at least both legs.

At meal times he would lift his backside away from the chair to allow the expelled wind to hit the air unhindered. His aim was to make a loud and disgusting noise; the louder it was and the more outrage it caused, the broader was his grin.

We three older children responded with silent revulsion, which only made things worse. We were not allowed to leave the table, hold our noses or turn away.

His smell was a potent memory and led to a growing distaste in all of us for bodily functions.

Madeleine holds the letter in her shaking hand. She lets it fall onto the sideboard, picks up the telephone receiver and dials. A man's voice answers. Damn, damn. She hangs up and dials again, slower this time. It's ringing. She is relieved to hear Lindy's voice say hello.

'Can you come down?'

'Of course. What's wrong?'

'I . . . they . . .'

Lindy can hear Madeleine crying.

'What's happened? Madeleine? Can you hear me?'

'Ye-s,' comes the reply, between sobs.

'I'll be right there.'

Lindy's lips move silently. She is repeating some of what Dr Kemble has written.

It has come to our attention . . .

. . . you are asked to present yourself at Rydalmere Psychiatric Centre for immediate admission . . .

. . . hopefully this will be for a short time only, while we assess your progress . . .

   . . . failure to admit yourself voluntarily will result in your being admitted under Schedule 2 of the Mental Health Act 1958, as amended.

She looks at Madeleine over the top of the page.

'I told John I didn't trust that man. He can't do this . . .'

Madeleine rocks back and forth, hugging her upper body with her arms. Christopher is playing on the floor. His bottom lip wobbles. He gets up and leans against Madeleine's knees, making whimpering sounds. She pulls him onto her lap, buries her face in his neck and strokes his back.

Practical as ever, Lindy strides into the kitchen. She has filled the kettle and is about to light the stove when she has an idea.

'That woman Dick works with – remember I told you about her? The one who had a breakdown?'

Madeleine lifts her head and nods. Christopher inspects his mother's face. She tweaks his nose. He giggles and struggles to get down. Lindy has abandoned the kettle. Hands on hips, she stands in the doorway and continues her story.

'Well, she's been going to this shrink fella somewhere in Croydon, I think. I could get his number from her. Maybe you could ring him and see if he can help?'

The afternoon passes quickly. She's been busy making phone calls. She collects Michael from school and stops on the way home to buy ice creams. She parks the car in the driveway. Christopher gives her a sticky kiss as she helps him out of the back seat. She hasn't phoned John to tell him about the letter; he doesn't like phone calls at work, and besides he may not even be there. She'll tell him tonight. She sets up the ironing board and brings a pile of folded washing in from the laundry. Michael and Christopher are watching television. The iron is plugged in. While it gets hot she sorts through the children's clothing.

Unexpectedly, John comes home around four o'clock. He greets her with a shame-faced expression.

'You were right about my leg. Dr Gardiner says the ulcer is a bit of a worry. My blood-sugar level's up too. He's arranging for me to be admitted to hospital this afternoon.'

Madeleine thumps the iron down on the ironing board. She's worried she might drop it. John rushes on. He thinks he knows what she's going to say.

'Don't worry, I've let them know at work, and Wally says he can arrange for you to collect my pay on Thursday.'

The panic starts up again. Madeleine clutches at the collar of her dress. Everything is happening too fast.

'I've had a letter from Dr Kemble . . .'

She joins him at the kitchen table. Her hands won't stay still. She rubs one inside the other. It takes a while to tell the whole story.

'. . . and there's this Dr Williams, he's a psychiatrist too. He says he can get me into this private hospital where he admits his patients, it's at Ashfield, it means I won't have to go back to Rydalmere.'

There's a pleading look on her face. She is wringing her hands. A faint rasping sound accompanies each movement.

'But he says you have to phone Kemble, otherwise the police can be sent here to get me.'

John rubs the back of his head with frantic finger strokes.

'What about the kids? Mum can't take them again – she's getting too old. Do you reckon Lindy would?'

Her voice is strangled, desperate.

'I don't know, John, I don't know. I can't solve every

bloody problem. You do something. Get on to Kemble and tell him I've got a new doctor. I'm not going back into that place, do you hear me? I'm not going back there, John, I'll . . . I'll . . .'

John's fingers move in circles on the top of his scalp.

'OK, OK, calm down. You know Kemble won't like this. Tell me again what this new bloke said. How long will you have to be in hospital? Do we have to pay him ourselves, or can we claim on the medical fund? Bloody hell, this could cost me a fortune.'

Dr Kemble is not available when John rings. The woman he speaks to says she knows about the letter and, well, the matter is out of her hands. Perhaps the children will have to go into care? Does John want to speak to the social worker? If he would just like to hang on a moment, she'll transfer him.

Minutes later, John puts down the phone. He sighs deeply.

Madeleine is impatient.

'We've got twenty-four hours to arrange everything. You'd better ring Dr Gardiner and tell him I can't go into hospital today.'

Next morning Madeleine doesn't trust herself to drive the car. She walks Michael to school. He is unusually chatty and doesn't seem to notice she's not listening to him. Outside the classroom door she breaks down and tells his teacher, Mrs McKenzie, what is happening.

'. . . I don't even know how long I'll be in there,' she sobs in a whisper, watching Michael run along the corridor. She is worried he'll hear her. She doesn't know how she's going to tell him he has to go into a home. The very thought of her children left in the care of strangers makes her sick with anxiety.

As she walks back home along familiar streets, her mind is in turmoil. Should she take the boys and run? Where would she go?

She steps through the front door just as John puts down the phone. Christopher is hanging on to the cord.

'That was the school. Sister Gertrude said Mrs McKenzie would take the boys, but I told her it's all been arranged.'

'You said what? Are you stupid? For God's sake, John, ring her back. No, you dial the number, I'll speak to her myself.'

Late that afternoon Madeleine drives John to Liverpool Hospital. The children wave goodbye at the door of his ward. Next stop Cabramatta. Judith McKenzie and her husband Clem are waiting. Lamingtons are on the table, and biscuits and milk for Michael and Christopher. A suitcase of clothes is whisked into the spare bedroom. Clem carries in a few extra bits and pieces.

'Do you always carry this much stuff?'

His question is softened by a good-humoured laugh.

Over cups of tea the adults talk. Judith and Clem are keen to impress on Madeleine their good intentions. They both love children; they've been trying to start a family for years. Judith is sure she can cope.

'Sister Gertrude has been a great help. She said young Christopher here' – Judith pauses to give him a smile – 'can join the kindergarten class during school time, and Clem can get time off if necessary.'

'We're happy to help,' Clem insists.

'I'd hate to see them taken into care,' Judith adds.

Clem helps Michael unpack his cars, and Judith beams with pleasure when Christopher shows no objection to sitting on her lap. Deliberately, Madeleine keeps her goodbyes to the children brief, resisting the temptation to rush back and kiss them one last time.

She has already explained as much as she can to Michael. Walking home from school with him, she had discussed her illness in words she hoped he would understand.

'Mummy has a sore head, a bit like a car that's broken down. I have to go into hospital and get it fixed.'

Driving down the Hume Highway, she stops at the lights at Villawood. She can see Michael's solemn face vividly, and his concerned reply rings in her ears.

'But Mummy, sometimes cars can't be fixed. They break down for good and have to be towed away . . .'

A brass plate on each door indicates the room number. There are no wards here. Madeleine is given the bed under the window. Two of the other patients in Room 3 have hired TV sets. The fourth bed is not made up.

Nurse Simpson continues the tour.

'Along here is the bathroom. You can have a bath or a shower, and the toilets are over there.'

She points to a sliding door.

Back in the corridor, Nurse Simpson opens a door halfway down. Wood panelling makes the room seem smaller than it is. The chairs all have straight backs and padded leather seats. There is no other furniture.

'A senior staff member runs a meeting in here every second day. It's part of your treatment. Patients can air their views, make complaints or suggest an activity, that sort of thing.'

The next room is larger. The timber panelling here is only waist high. The upper half of all four walls is made of glass. Several low, comfy chairs are grouped around coffee tables. There's a book on the arm of a chair, a used mug near by. Nurse Simpson strokes the fabric on the back of a chair.

'This is the patients' lounge. They're all at dinner at the moment, in case you're wondering why no one's around. Have you eaten?'

'Yes, I had something a short while ago, thanks very much.'

'You'll find the food good. We have two cooks, and they've been with us for years.'

She smiles warmly.

'It's still a hospital, of course, but we do our best to make it feel like home.'

Through a door and down a spiral staircase, a cement path leads from a small garden to a building that looks like an enormous garage. The words OCCUPATIONAL THERAPY ROOM are painted on the door. Inside, Madeleine can see piles of paper and cardboard. A long wooden work table, splattered with dried paint and glue, runs almost the full length of the room. A number of wooden stools line the table on both sides.

'Not everyone feels able to talk about their problems. Some like to make things. We have one man here who makes toys for his grandchildren. Very good they are too.'

Nurse Simpson checks her watch.

'We'd better hurry. Dr Williams is expecting you. No, this way. His rooms are right next door.'

Madeleine closes the gate behind her. The dark brick veranda has a stone arch and floor tiles. Her aunt used to have a house with a veranda like this one. The door is similar too. Glass squares in a wooden frame. A curtain has been fitted to the inside of the door. Madeleine can remember her aunt's curtain was made of net, gathered top and bottom on a length of dowel. If you put your face up close you could peep through.

'Come in, come in, Mrs Roberts. It's good to meet you. Thanks, Emily – oh, hang on a minute . . .'

He turns back to Madeleine.

'Do you want Emily to come back for you, or can you find your own way back?'

'I think I can,' Madeleine replies nervously, mentally following the route along the cement path.

Dr Williams indicates a chair alongside his desk.

'I'm due home in ten minutes – it's my daughter's birthday – but I wanted to meet you first. I've spoken to Dr Kemble. He's sending me a copy of your treatment notes and a report on your medical history. In the mean time I'm going to take you off all medication. Is there anything you'd like to ask?'

'I don't really understand why I'm here. This neighbour, the one who made the complaint, she . . .'

Dr Williams pulls a tissue from the box on his desk. He hands it to Madeleine.

'You're here now, so let's not worry. I'll speak to you tomorrow. I want you to come and see me at 10 a.m. The nursing staff know, but we like to make patients responsible for their own appointments, OK?'

Madeleine blows her nose on the tissue. She feels exhausted. It is an effort to stand up and walk to the door. She pushes open the gate and steps onto the cement path.

Twenty-four patients are gathered in the wood-panelled room. Dr Williams' offsider, Kerry Symes, is running things today. Dr Symes has problems with his spectacles. He is continually pushing them higher up on the bridge of his nose, pointing his index finger between his eyebrows, like a man about to shoot his brains out. He favours tightly fitting blue striped shirts and loud ties with unusually small knots. His shirt is damp under the armpits. Madeleine imagines he smells of sweat. She chooses a chair some distance away; she's already decided she doesn't like Dr Symes.

A Christian Brother is the last patient to arrive. He smiles hello around the room, takes the chair on Madeleine's left and introduces himself. Brother Damian. Madeleine starts counting. There are six brothers in the room now, and four priests, but only two nuns.

Madeleine has never thought of nuns and priests and brothers breaking down or having problems like ordinary people. At school she often used to wonder about the nuns. They lived in a walled-up world of prayer and patient serenity. Did they ever get angry or shout? She didn't think so. And what about their feet? Were those black boots the sort you could buy in a shoe shop? Probably not. They must have been taught how to walk the minute they entered the convent. It didn't look like walking. Madeleine searches around for the right word. Glide, yes, that's it. They glided. Maybe they operated on a different plane, where conveyor belts did the work of feet? Their eyes were a bit odd too, glazed over and vaguely distracted, as if they were listening intently. Were they listening to the faint murmurings of their shared husband? Strange to think Jesus was – what's the term? – polygamous. More of an idea or a belief than a flesh-and-blood husband who pinched all the bedclothes and left the bathroom in a mess. Did He say the same things to each of them? Exactly how many? How many Catholic countries were there? That would be a good counting job. Madeleine pictures herself in front of a rostrum, recounting statistics to a large audience.

'At the last count Jesus Christ, the man who never married but gained a harem here on earth after He'd returned to Heaven, had seven thousand, five hundred and sixty-two wives. Of these, nine hundred and eighty-seven have removed their wedding bands and returned to everyday life. They did not need to attend a court hearing, and of course there were no children, so no need for a custody hearing either. However, they did need the permission of His Holiness, the Pope, who was said to be bitterly disappointed.'

Maybe he was disappointed because he had no wives?

Brother Damian prods Madeleine gently with his elbow. Dr Symes is talking to her. She looks beyond the doctor's shoulder at the wooden panelling.

'I'm sorry, Doctor, could you repeat that?'

'I asked if you had any thoughts about what sort of treatment you would prefer?'

She looks at him blankly. How should she know?

Brother Damian puts up his hand.

Dr Symes acknowledges the interruption with a nod of his head.

Brother Damian clears his throat.

'Could you outline for all of us what the suggestions are?'

Dr Symes pulls at his tie, stretching his neck above the tight knot.

'I thought we might get away from the usual talk-talk type therapy and try something a little different. Psychodrama, for example.'

'What's that?' asks the male patient sitting near the door.

'It's a kind of role play, where each of you acts out yourself in a particular situation, and another patient or a member of staff, say, plays the real-life characters you interact with. Maybe it's your wife or husband, or' – hastily he corrects himself – 'a friend or colleague with whom you have daily or at least regular contact.'

The man near the door is looking bored.

'What's the point?'

Dr Symes is waving his tie around. He stands up and grapples with the knot, his chin high in the air. An elderly man is transfixed by Dr Symes' antics.

'Is that what you mean by role play, Doctor?'

'No, it isn't,' comes the agitated reply.

The tie is off. Dr Symes folds it neatly and shoves it in his back trouser pocket.

'I'm going to put two notices on the board outside,' he announces, getting ready for a quick getaway. 'Put your name on the appropriate list, and do it soon. I'll be back on Friday and we'll talk about it again then.'

He's out the door before they have time to protest. Disappointment shows on at least three faces, and the priest next to Madeleine still has his hand up.

Breakfast time is noisy. Plates and bowls clatter on the long wooden tables. Voices echo across the room. Madeleine likes to wait until the last possible moment, anxious to avoid any attempts at conversation. Brother Damian sits down opposite her. His smile is conspiratorial. He likes to come late too.

She jumps up to pour them both mugs of tea from the big silver pot on the table. He reaches for the jug of milk.

As she stirs her tea, Madeleine wishes she could get up and walk away.

'Can I ask you a question?' Brother Damian says.

Startled, she raises her head.

'Y-es.'

'Do I make you feel uncomfortable?'

'Of course not . . . I mean, yes, you do. No, I mean it's not you, it's . . .'

'It's the way we've been taught to think about the church? Is that what you mean?'

This time she looks him full in the face. His eyes are a greeny brown colour. There's a lingering sadness in them that makes him look as though he's about to cry. She's amazed to see her right hand reach out and touch the fingers curled around his mug of tea.

'I'm sorry,' she says.

....

Nurse Corrigan shows the couple into Room 3. The woman looks around.

'There she is, Reggie. C'mon.'

That voice. Madeleine looks up from her chair.

'Mum, what are you doing here?'

Jessie has the warmth of the sun in her face. She beams golden rays in her daughter's direction, tapping the side of her nose with one finger. She's canny about getting information, don't you know? But then she always was.

'Ways and means, my darling. How are you? Let me introduce my fi-a-ncé.'

Jessie drags the word out, making it special.

'Reggie, this is Madeleine, my youngest girl. She's the bright one, won a scholarship when she was twelve.'

She pulls away from Reggie's arm and pushes him forward, her outspread hand in the small of his back. His eyes drop to the floor.

'Howdja do.'

Madeleine doesn't bother returning his greeting. She's already dismissed him as a fool. So what's this one? Husband number five or six?

'How long has it been?' Jessie muses.

Madeleine's reply is prompt. She knows the answer.

'Thirteen years.'

'Not that long, surely. And have you forgiven me yet?'

Sunbeams play around Jessie's lips, and her eyebrows are arched in mock surprise.

Madeleine shrugs her shoulders. That all depends. Her attention is caught, as it was constantly throughout her childhood, by the tiny nodule of raised flesh that sits perched on the tip of her mother's nose. Is it a wart? A pimple? Neither is a satisfactory definition, but it is just as she remembers it, clogged with face powder, her mother's attempt to camouflage its size. She was about ten when she first noticed it, really saw it for the first time. From that day on she had pleaded with the Virgin Mary to make sure she didn't grow up with a wart on her nose. Her prayers were answered, sort of. Maybe God's hand slipped? The domed nodule on her upper lip is smaller and smoother than Jessie's, but she can see now how similar they are. It's a family heirloom, the only present her mother is ever likely to give her. Madeleine smiles ruefully at the thought, and Jessie is pleased.

'We'll make up for lost time, love. I'll help you get well and Reggie wants to get to know you, don't you, Reggie?'

She looks at him expectantly. He shuffles from one foot to the other. Nurse Corrigan comes bustling through the door.

'I'm sorry, Madeleine, your visitors will have to leave. It's almost lunchtime.'

Jessie's voice takes on a theatrical formality.

'It was so nice of you to allow us to see my daughter, Nurse. I can't tell you how much I appreciate it.'

Madeleine wonders if Nurse Corrigan is taken in by her mother's false charm. Most people are.

'I'm sure Madeleine was thrilled to see you.'

Madeleine rolls 'thrilled' around on her tongue.

The light is shining in her face. The nurse speaks in a hoarse whisper.

'Put your dressing gown on, Mrs Roberts, and come with me. Dr Williams is waiting in the lounge.'

'Is it my children? Is something wrong?'

'Shh. I honestly don't know. Here, let me help you.'

Madeleine can't find her slippers. The nurse directs the torch towards the floor, playing the beam around the bed. Oh, there they are. Together Madeleine and the nurse walk down the corridor. Dr Williams comes towards them. His hand grips Madeleine's elbow, and he guides her to the nearest chair.

'Thank you Nurse. Are you warm enough, Madeleine?'

'Is it Christopher? Has he hurt himself?'

'No. No. As far as I know your children are fine.'

Madeleine isn't convinced.

'I rang them tonight, and Judith said everything was fine. John? Is it John?'

'No, let me tell you.'

He takes her hand in both of his.

'You have a brother, don't you?'

'Two. Tim and Eddy.'

He looks puzzled.

'I'm sorry, I don't know which one it is . . .'

He releases her hand, gets up and opens the door. The nurse is waiting outside.

'Can you phone this number?' He takes a piece of paper from his shirt pocket. 'Ask for Dr Jeremy Cooper. Tell him I want to know the name. Got that?'

The nurse hurries off.

Tim or Eddy? Tim. It was bound to be him. They used to be so close. He was the big brother she looked up to. She'd been appalled when she saw the bruises on Janine's face. Maybe he'd gone too far? Maybe Janine was dead?

Dr Williams is still in the corridor. She can hear him talking to the nurse. He comes back into the room and closes the door.

'I'm very sorry, Madeleine, I didn't want to go on till I'd checked the details. The doctor who rang me was from Gladesville Hospital. I suppose you know Tim was a patient there?'

She didn't know. The look on her face tells him that. He pulls a chair up close and sits down. His knees are almost touching hers.

'Dr Cooper tells me he was in and out of hospital all last year, suffering from depression after his marriage broke up. I understand he was in the army?'

'Yes, he was a kid when he joined up. He's dead, isn't he?'

'I'm afraid he is. He committed suicide. I'm so very sorry.'

'When?'

'Around 7 p.m. tonight. It took them a while to locate your whereabouts. He had you down as next of kin.

Apparently the police heard from one of your neighbours that you were here. I asked them to let me tell you myself.'

'So John doesn't know yet?'

'I wouldn't have thought so.'

Dr Williams studies Madeleine's face carefully. She is calm, unemotional, almost too calm.

'The funeral is on Thursday. Will you want to go?'

'Yes, of course.'

'All right then. I'll give you some medication to help you get through the day and something to make you sleep tonight. Is there anyone you can ask to go with you? I'd be happy to phone and explain if you like . . .'

'No, thank you, Dr Williams. I can ask him myself.'

A sleek black car pulls into the hospital driveway. The driver opens the back door. Nurse Simpson and Brother Damian help Madeleine onto the back seat. She giggles and her speech is slurred.

'My mummy must have found herself a rich boyfriend this time.'

Brother Damian sits beside her. He giggles too.

'What poisonous potion have you sipped?'

'Dunno. They gave me an injection after breakfast. I feel like a drunk, only worse.'

Her head lolls around, and she has to hold on tight to prevent herself from sliding to one side. Brother Damian wedges her right side against his arm.

'How do you feel?' he asks.

'Odd. I can think OK, but my body doesn't seem to belong to me. I don't think I could walk on my own.'

'Maybe they gave you the dose for an elephant?'

She giggles again.

'That's 'cos I never forget.'

'Me neither. A symptom of our illness, would you say?'

Jessie is waiting on the footpath. There's someone with her – not Reggie, someone else. Madeleine is unable to focus her eyes on the stranger, but she knows who it is. *Him*. Albert. She has referred to this man as *him* ever since she was sixteen years old. Why did he have to come, anyway? Tim's not his son. He never wanted any of them. 'You're here on sufferance,' he'd say, that mean bottom lip curling, spitting out the words. Except for Edward. He'd never say such a thing to Edward, no, not to his only precious son.

Brother Damian runs round the back of the car. The driver has the door open, but Madeleine makes no move to get out. She is slumped back against the seat, her eyes glazed, and there's a grey look about her.

'She'll be next,' Albert comments to Jessie.

Madeleine doesn't let on she has heard.

Using both hands, she presses her fingers tightly into the flesh either side of her left knee and lifts her leg out of the car. Her shoe touches the footpath, but she can't feel anything. Now the other leg. Brother Damian pulls her upwards towards him and half-carries, half-drags her to the church door. Gratefully she sinks into the nearest pew.

People file past. No one recognises Madeleine. She tells herself she doesn't care. The coffin is in the middle of the aisle, further down, close to the altar. There's a wreath of flowers on top. She thinks about Tim and remembers the polite, sometimes withdrawn boy, with a wry sense of humour and a lopsided grin. Could he have guessed she'd respond to his death as though it were a parting gift? Something momentous has happened to her in the past forty-eight hours.

Tim's father had been Jessie's second husband, and he'd committed suicide too. Tim once told Madeleine how he'd gone in search of his aunt, his father's only sister. It had been easy to find her – she still lived in the same suburb, and her name was in the phone book. She'd told Tim his father had committed suicide the same night he discovered his wife in bed with Albert. A few months after that night, when Tim was four and Lizzie almost two, Albert had married Jessie and so became husband number three. Madeleine was born later that year.

Tim had always pooh-poohed the idea of children. 'Who in their right mind would want brats running around?' he'd ask whenever Madeleine brought up the subject. Now, suddenly, she thinks she sees another dimension to his decision. Was the idea of suicide a legacy that was passed on? Did that idea get into your blood? Maybe it hung over you, suspended in time, waiting for a weak moment? What impact would her suicide have had on her sons? A shiver runs down the length of her spine. She couldn't do it to them, she simply couldn't. Not now.

The coffin is carried out the door. Madeleine is aware of people milling around outside the church. Her body is heavy. She leans against Brother Damian and speaks briefly to her mother. No, she won't go to the cemetery; she needs to get back to the hospital.

Shaking her head slightly, mournfully, Jessie blinks and keeps her eyes closed a fraction longer than is necessary. She blinks again. Another long moment. She is the grief-stricken mother burying her elder son, and a suicide at that.

Madeleine wants to nudge Brother Damian in the ribs, to burst out laughing in her mother's face.

The slow blinks are finished. Jessie moves closer.

'It's such a comfort, Brother, knowing my daughter is in such good hands.'

She takes his hand, but instead of shaking it she puts it to her lips.

'Please take good care of her. God knows, I've suffered enough for three lifetimes already, I can't take any more . . .'

She presses her lips against his fingers in a devout kiss.

'. . . but it's people like you and the rest of your staff that give me the strength to go on.'

There is a twitch at one corner of Brother Damian's mouth, but he maintains his composure. He disengages his hand awkwardly and manoeuvres himself and Madeleine closer to the sleek black car. Madeleine's head droops onto her chest. She hopes no one can see her shaking with silent laughter.

On the way back to the hospital the driver checks his rear-vision mirror. What are those two up to? They're rolling around on the back seat like a couple of kids. He'd thought the bloke was all right, but look at him — he's as loopy as she is! Fruit cakes, both of 'em. You get some queer types in this business, that's for sure.

'I haven't laughed . . .'

Brother Damian struggles to finish the sentence. Tears stream down his face. He doubles up, holding his stomach.

'I've got a pain, I haven't laughed so much . . .'

'I know, I know,' Madeleine replies.

He straightens in his seat.

'You must think I'm awful, laughing at your family.'

'No. I think today I learnt, finally, how to deal with them. If you could have seen your face! I thought she was gonna call you Saint Damian.'

They're off again. Madeleine catches the driver's look in

the rear-vision mirror. She pulls faces at him, screwing up her mouth and nose, making herself look like the lunatic he imagines her to be.

On Friday morning Madeleine wakes from a disturbing dream. There are tears in her eyes. Gingerly she eases herself out of bed. Her head feels as if it's been stuffed with cotton wool. Under the shower her sobs are drowned out by the hot hiss of water. She's the last one to arrive for breakfast, and the only one left in the dining room when the kitchen staff begin clearing tables. Rummaging around for coins in her handbag, she stands in line for the phone.

She speaks briefly to the matron in John's ward, then checks the noticeboard in the corridor. Among an array of leaflets and handwritten prayers pinned corner-style, looking like they've been there for some time, a sheet of paper signed by Dr Symes has a prominent place. There are two columns and two headings. DISCUSSION THERAPY is the first heading. The column space below is filled up with a long list of names. Hers is the only name in the right-hand column, under the heading PSYCHODRAMA. She pushes open the door of the meeting room. Dr Symes frowns at her late arrival.

'Have you not got a watch, Madeleine?'

Her tone is as abrupt at his.

'My husband is in hospital. I had to phone and see how he was.'

'And couldn't that have waited till afterwards?'

'No, it couldn't.'

She looks around for Brother Damian. He is not in the room. Was his name on the list?

Dr Symes sighs with impatience.

'If we can just get on.'

Madeleine can't keep still. She leans forward, and her eyes glare round the room.

'I want to say something.'

'Go on, then.'

'I think you're all piss weak. You said we'd try something different' – she throws a stony glance at Dr Symes – 'but I'm the only one who put my name down for this psychodrama stuff. What's wrong with the rest of you? Are you too scared to take a closer look at yourselves?'

A woman puts up her hand.

'Yes, Frances?'

Dr Symes smiles. He's beginning to enjoy himself.

'I don't like Madeleine's attitude.'

'I don't either,' adds one of the priests.

Dr Symes makes a suggestion.

'Shall we take a vote?'

Frances is confused.

'What are we to vote about?'

Dr Symes crosses his arms and nods his head in Madeleine's direction.

'Does Madeleine stay, or shall we ask her to leave?'

A chorus of voices agrees to the suggestion.

'Yeah, let's vote.'

'Good idea.'

Hostility is in the air. Dr Symes hasn't seen this much animation in ages. Patients are invariably too timid and polite.

He instructs them to say yes or no. Yes means Madeleine can stay; vote no and she'll be asked to leave. He begins with the male patient near the door.

'Tom?'

Dr Symes goes round the room, indicating each person's turn with a pointed index finger.

'No.'

'No.'

'No.'

'No.'

Madeleine is keeping tally. Ten against. That's quite enough, thank you. On shaky legs she heads for the door.

A new patient, George Elston, rises to his feet. He's a big man, and his bulk gives him a commanding appearance. His shoulders are massive. He used to be a footballer. They say he almost killed a man once. George has only been in this joint two days, and already he's feeling like a fish out of water, but one thing his father taught him was to stand up and be counted. His voice is gruff. He's a man of few words.

'The only sane person who was in this room just left. And I think the lady's right, you are all piss weak.'

He walks past Dr Symes. Softly he mutters out of the side of his mouth, 'You too, Doc.'

In the craft room, Nurse Simpson helps Madeleine and George to make flowers. George has made three roses already. His long, thick fingers move quickly, deftly. He has a flair for this kind of thing. Madeleine is still on her first flower. She twists a length of wire around the stem, but the crepe paper keeps unravelling. Annoyed, she throws the tangled mess onto the table.

'Can I go back to my room, Nurse?'

'No, but those shelves behind you need sorting. See what you can do with them.'

Madeleine works busily. Later she makes cups of tea for everyone and hands around the biscuit tin. Nurse Simpson is up the back of the room, sorting through order forms. She takes a biscuit and places a restraining hand on Madeleine's wrist.

'I know you're angry, Madeleine, but think for a moment – maybe you're further along in your recovery than many of the others in that group?'

Angry? What a thought.

She feels a rush of warmth for this woman.

'Thank you for pointing that out. I really didn't know what to think.'

She's in the garden early next morning, tracking a slow circle, enjoying the warmth of the sun. Her head feels clearer than it has for years. The cloud of depression that usually sits around her shoulders has retreated. She's Alice in Wonderland, tall enough to reach above the clouds, to see what's going on.

Picking up a stone, she holds it in her fingers, rubbing its smoothness with her thumb. She has made her mind up about a few things. What's more, she isn't going to tell anyone.

She spits on the stone, then looks about for a place to bury it. I'm never coming back here, Stone. I'm getting out of this place and I'm gonna prove to myself that I can live my life differently. Right now I can't do that for myself, but I can do it for my kids.

The soil is loose beneath a gardenia bush. She digs around with her hands and places the stone, wet side up, in the hole, covering it with soil, patting it into place.

Five seconds before 2 p.m. Five, four, three, two, one, go. She knocks on the familiar glass door. She has been rehearsing all morning. Her tone has to be just right, firm but reasonable.

Dr Williams holds up his hand in mock protest.

'Hold on there a moment, it's early days yet.'

'I don't think so. I've been here almost four weeks. I want to be with my children.'

'And John?'

She answers as though she has misunderstood his question.

'We think he'll be discharged some time next week.'

'Have they adjusted his insulin?'

'I'm not sure. I think the ulcer on his leg was the real problem.'

Dr Williams fiddles with papers on his desk. He keeps his voice light.

'Does John manage his diabetes well?'

Madeleine hesitates before replying. Can she trust this man? Should she take the risk? Once she begins to speak, the words spill out with a life of their own.

'I don't think he's ever accepted it. He says he can't give up the beer, especially when he's with his mates. He eats lots of ice cream too. I can't talk to him about it . . .'

She pauses and her voice drops to a whisper.

'Trouble is, I can't talk to him about *anything*.'

Dr Williams runs his teeth across his bottom lip. Madeleine has noticed that he does this a lot. She understands he is thinking. He scratches behind one ear with the end of his pen.

'I'd like to suggest that I see you two together for a few sessions. An hour, maybe two. Get you talking to each other. Do you think he would come?'

'I'm not sure, but I hope he'll agree.'

'Good. Good.'

Dr Williams pushes back his chair. He walks around his desk and sits on the corner nearest to Madeleine's chair.

'Were you ever told the diagnosis you'd been given, Madeleine?'

'My husband told me.'

'Did he now? And what did he tell you?'

She drops her eyes.

'I'm a paranoid schizophrenic.'

'Yes, that is what they'd decided, but I don't agree.'

Madeleine's eyes rake his face.

'You don't?'

'No. I think you're a manic depressive.'

'Oh.'

. . . .

It's one week later. Madeleine has driven straight to Liverpool Hospital. John puts his suitcase on the back seat and opens the passenger door for her. He adjusts the rear-vision mirror before turning on the ignition.

'Judith said they'll come about seven. I wanted to pick the boys up sooner, but I could tell she was finding it hard.'

John drives out of the hospital gates.

'And what's this about your mother getting married?'

'Yeah, next Saturday. The reception is at Reggie's RSL Club. They aren't having a church wedding. She wants to meet everyone at the reception. Some friends of Reggie's are gonna be the witnesses, she said.'

'She sure gets around, doesn't she?'

'Tim used to call her Liz Taylor. All those husbands. This bloke is number five.'

John pulls up at a red light.

'I could understand it if she was a good sort.'

Madeleine feels a stab of irritation. She counts to ten, then backwards to one. Her voice is cool.

'Takes all types.'

A few minutes later he pulls into their driveway.

'Isn't it good to be home?'

He unlocks the front door and carries their bags inside. Madeleine puts the kettle on while John sorts through a pile of mail Lindy has left on the sideboard. There's a dozen red roses nicely arranged in a vase. Madeleine fingers a petal, remembering the feel of crepe paper. George will probably open a fake flower shop soon.

'I hoped we might talk before the boys came back, John . . .'

He plonks the mail onto the kitchen table and looks through the window.

'Great idea, love, but look at that grass, I'll have to run the mower over it right away.'

Judith is helping Madeleine to get the children ready for bed. If Michael can get into his pyjamas quick as a wink, Clem will read him a story.

'Do you feel you've benefited from being in hospital?' Judith asks tentatively.

Madeleine smiles ruefully before answering.

'Yes and no. It's hard to explain. I still have to cope with the likes of her across the road . . .' – she indicates the direction of Cora's house with a jerk of her thumb – '. . . and not react. Dr Williams says it's important to be a person and not an emotional reaction. I want to remember that. I'm thinking I might look for a job.'

Judith eases Christopher's arm into his pyjama top. He's bouncing up and down on the kitchen table. Madeleine drinks in the sight of him as Judith begins on the buttons.

'What sort of work?'

'Office work if I could get it, but I'd consider anything.'

'I usually work at the local RSL club at weekends. I'm due to start back there next Saturday. I could ask if they have any vacancies, if you like.'

'What would I do there?'

'I'm on the front desk, but there's also a self-serve cafeteria and the bar's busy all the time.'

'I've never worked in a bar before. Would they train me?'

Judith tickles Christopher's belly.

'Probably.'

'It sounds ideal, but don't worry, I'm not expecting miracles.'

'Do you have to see the doctor again?'

'Oh yes, but one of the nurses gave me a leaflet about this group called SHEPP – Self Help for Ex-Psychiatric Patients. I might go to one of their meetings.'

'That sounds like a good idea. A bit like AA?'

'I don't know, I suppose so.'

Madeleine leans forward with Christopher in her arms, offering him to Judith for a goodnight kiss. Together the two women walk into his room. Judith watches Madeleine tuck him into his cot.

'They're lovely children, Madeleine. I couldn't help wishing at times that they were mine.'

Madeleine closes the door behind her and follows Judith down the hall.

'Like I said before, they can come and stay with you again. I'd like to think there were other people who loved them. I've got no family, and John's mother is getting on . . .'

'We'd like that, Clem, wouldn't we?'

Clem slams the nursery-rhyme book shut and grins at Michael.

'Yeah, we sure would, wouldn't we, mate?'

Judith signals to her husband.

'We'd better go. Where's John? I don't want to leave without saying goodbye.'

Madeleine hurries over to the back door.

It's dark outside. She can't see John, but she can guess where he is. She shouts out his name.

'John.'

He throws down the hose and turns off the tap. Bounding up the back steps, he rushes past Madeleine and into the house. His grin is sheepishly apologetic.

'Sorry, everyone, The orchids are in such a mess. It'll take at least a week to get things back to normal.'

....

She gags the moment the first tablet touches her tongue. Heaving, she spits it into the sink. Imagine eating seven bloody teaspoonfuls of salt every morning. That's what these seven Lithium tablets taste like. Many years later, she'll find out that Lithium was given to soldiers during the Second World War as a salt substitute. Madeleine has to have a blood test every six weeks to check the Lithium levels in her blood.

The first tablet is down. She puts the second one in her mouth, swallowing quickly so as not to taste it. She must have a slingshot down there somewhere, because almost immediately the tablets hit the back of her throat and come flying past her lips like bullets. They land in the sink. She rinses out her mouth and puts the remaining tablets back in the bottle. That's it for today. She'll try again tomorrow.

The same thing happens the next day and the one after

that. She simply can't get them down. Now the mere sight of the bottle turns her stomach. She imagines a passageway inside her, running in a straight line from her throat to her belly. Each time she swallows a tablet, that passageway gets wider, making it easier for her stomach to react with a catapult action.

She tries various ways to get them down. With milk, after meals, last thing at night – the result is always the same. Finally she understands it's her body that's making the decision. She can't take this stuff. Her body won't let her. There's another five weeks before she has to have the blood test. What she'll do then, she still doesn't know.

Michael and Christopher are eating ice creams. Lindy stands with them at her front gate and inspects John's new car.

'It's nice, John,' she says.

'About time too. I've been working there long enough.'

'Will they let you keep it all the time?' Lindy asks.

'Yeah. The boss said, so long as I look after it, it's all mine.'

Christopher's mouth is ringed with chocolate, and a sticky brown trickle runs down his hand. Michael licks daintily and often, rotating the cone all the while.

'I don't think I'll risk another kiss,' says Madeleine with a chuckle, manoeuvring herself past Christopher and into the car. John honks the horn as they drive off to the RSL club for Jessie's big day.

There's a darn in Madeleine's patio dress. Someone must have dropped ash the last time she wore it. She's never been good with needle and thread, but the vivid floral design makes it hard to detect her stitching. Lindy has lent her a handbag, which is some consolation for her scuffed white shoes.

The RSL club is on a corner, positioned well back from the main road. Judith is behind the front desk.

'I was hoping you might be here,' Madeleine says with a bright smile.

'I was going to ring you. Guess what?'

'I don't know. Tell me. What?'

'One of the girls who works with me has left. I put in a good word for you. Gerry, he's the boss, said for you to give him a ring.'

John looks from Madeleine to Judith and back to Madeleine.

'What's this?'

Madeleine winks at him. 'I'll tell you about it in a minute.' She turns her face away from him. Judith picks up the warning and chooses her words carefully.

'He's here at the moment. He might even decide to talk to you tonight. I know he's keen to solve the problem as soon as possible.'

On their way up the stairs Madeleine explains her plan to John. If she can work the odd weekend they might be able to save some money. Didn't he say last night how worried he was about making ends meet?

'. . . besides, I probably won't get it anyway.'

She feels distanced from the people around her, like a fly on the wall. Reggie is already the worse for drink, and Jessie looks like a painted doll, like one of those celluloid kewpie dolls they used to sell on sticks at the Royal Easter Show, with tizzy wings and huge eyes, an expression of frozen surprise fixed into place above an absurd grin.

When the toasts are over Madeleine slips away to the ladies' room. She's in the toilet when she hears two women talking. She thinks she recognises one of the voices. Isn't that the woman Reggie introduced her to earlier? Sally? Madeleine can hear the door of the next cubicle opening and closing. The women continue their conversation. Madeleine has worked out that Sally is the one in the loo.

'. . . a bit of a laugh, really. She's got her head screwed on, I tell you.'

'Do you think she loves him?'

'If she did she'd have married him, wouldn't she?'

'But she did marry him.'

Sally is pulling toilet paper off the roll. A moment later there's the sound of water flushing in the toilet bowl. The door opens again. Madeleine is tense with anxiety. She's concerned the women will wonder who's in her cubicle.

Sally's voice is faint against the background sound of running water. Madeleine leans forward, straining to hear.

'There was no wedding. She's moved in with him all right, but I know for a fact that she's hung on to her pension flat. Insurance, she reckons, in case it doesn't work out.'

'Did she actually say that?'

'Yeah, but not in front of Reggie.'

'But why go to all this trouble? I mean it's a bit rich arranging a reception . . .'

The women have gone. Madeleine's mind is racing. Lies and secrets, it's always been that way. And what is her role? Historian? Family detective? Always trying to understand, to get to the truth. Maybe there is no truth? Why bother trying to understand anyway? It isn't going to change anything.

John looks troubled.

'Where were you? You've been gone for ages.'

'I've probably eaten something that didn't agree with me. Are you ready to go?'

'Sure, just let me finish my beer.'

Madeleine avoids her mother's outstretched arms.

'I'll damage your beautiful corsage,' she says, aiming a peck at Jessie's cheek.

'I'm so glad you came, Maddy . . .'

It's been a long time since her mother called her that. Maybe she's psychic? She probably knows this is goodbye. Will it be another thirteen years before they meet again?

Dr Williams doesn't ask about the Lithium. He's more interested in her and John.

'Did he have anything to say after I saw you both the other night?'

'No. John never does say much.'

'He's very well defended, Madeleine.'

She doesn't like to ask what he means, but the words jump around in her head like bouncing balls. White bouncing balls.

When she was little, Tim used to take her and Lizzie to three different picture shows every Saturday. Edward was still a baby then, and Madeleine was glad. She was the youngest – on Saturdays, at least.

Their programme was the same each week. First they saw the 11 a.m. show at the Regal in Oxford Street, then Tim bought them each a meat pie before the children's matinee began at the Coronet across the road. Then they'd go on to the Star theatre, around the corner and further along Bronte Road, to catch the Intermediate programme at 5 p.m. Often they were the first ones in the queue.

Jessie gave Tim enough money for the tickets and a bit extra for something to eat. She said the same thing every week as they went out the front gate.

'Now, don't you dare come home before 7.30, hear me?'

The Coronet organised balloon-blowing competitions on stage and lucky door prizes, and once Lizzie won a box of chocolates. There were cartoons and sing-alongs, and Madeleine was entranced by the white ball that bounced from one word to another, pausing only to indicate to the audience how long to hold each note.

Here we are again, happy as can be.

All good friends and jolly good company.

This time the white ball goes back and forth between two words — *well defended, well defended, well defended*. She could sing along, but she can't understand exactly what the words mean.

'Madeleine? Madeleine?'

'I'm sorry, Doctor, I drifted off.'

'Can I ask what you were thinking?'

'About Tim. Memories flood back at odd times — I can't stop them.'

'That's understandable, but was it something I said that acted as a trigger?'

She couldn't tell him. He'd probably think she was an idiot.

'No, it just happens.'

'We could talk about Tim next time if you wish. Are you feeling better than before?'

'Much better, I think. I started that job last week.'

'Oh yes, I forgot. Did you manage OK?'

She doesn't want to tell him how her legs shook, how hard it was to stand for so long.

'I got to use the mike.' Madeleine pulls a face and pretends she's holding a microphone. 'Mr Smith, Mr Smith, could you come to the front desk please.' She laughs. 'I quite enjoy that bit.'

'It will give you confidence, and that's a good thing.'

He looks at his watch.

'Now, you and John have an appointment for Wednesday night, so I'll see you again then.'

The SHEPP meeting is due to start. Madeleine hovers at the door, searching for a friendly face. It has taken a while to find the place. She wants to get back in the car and drive home. A car door slams behind her. A woman is walking up the path.

'You must be Madeleine,' says a hearty voice.

'Yes. Rosemary?'

'That's right. I'm glad you made it.'

Madeleine steps back to let Rosemary get to the door.

A man is leaning against the far wall. As soon as the light goes on he steps through the door and walks across to take a seat at the table. One or two others join him. Madeleine counts heads quickly. There are eleven people in the room. Rosemary pulls out a chair and gestures for Madeleine to take the seat alongside her.

One of the men is fidgeting in his seat; another paces the floor. Rosemary opens the meeting. They go round the table. Each person says their name and a little about themselves, and how they're feeling. The pacing man is David. He's on a new treatment, but he doesn't think it's helping him much. It takes him a long time to tell his story. He explains that his tongue is swollen, and he's been living on tinned soup.

Rosemary asks if there are any questions David wants to ask his doctor. He shakes his head and shrugs his shoulders. They all discuss the matter. Daphne makes a suggestion.

Why not write down the symptoms? Mark talks about what he said to *his* doctor. David is encouraged to keep a daily diary. He agrees to bring the diary to next week's meeting.

The fidgeting man is Max. He has just come out of hospital, again. Everyone laughs when he says that. Madeleine doesn't say much, but she listens intently. On the way home she savours the feeling of being among friends. Fancy Rosemary only being out of hospital eighteen months! Maybe next week she could discuss her reluctance to take Lithium?

Madeleine is four months pregnant. She hadn't planned on having another baby, but maybe it's just the thing she and John need to bring them close again. And being pregnant has solved her medication problem. Dr Williams agrees it's best if she can stay off the Lithium for the time being. She hasn't seen him for several weeks. These days she prefers to discuss her progress at the SHEPP meetings.

One Saturday morning she wakes in the dark. She's been having odd darting pains all night. Stifling a groan, she rushes outside to the toilet. There's a plastic bucket near the laundry door. She grabs the handle on her way past. Minutes later, she staggers back into the kitchen, holding the bucket close to her blood-soaked thighs.

She's still crouched over the bucket when John gets up a few hours later.

'I've lost the baby,' she tells him.

'Shall I call a doctor?'

'No. I think I'll be OK. Could you run me a bath?'

'Sure. Why don't you go back to bed?'

'I will. Can you get some breakfast for the kids?'

Around eleven she crawls out of bed. She's got to be at the club by one.

She's brushing her hair in front of the bathroom mirror when John comes in to wash his hands.

'Do I look all right?' she asks him.

'Sure. You know, that bloody side fence will have to be replaced soon. Those mongrel kids next door keep kicking it. I've a good mind to make Peter pay the bill.'

Madeleine leans against the wall for support. She looks at John as though she has never seen him before in her life.

'You really don't care, do you?'

'Don't care? What do you mean? What did I say wrong this time?'

At work she faints. Gerry insists on driving her to the hospital himself. The doctor in Casualty is blunt. She'll need a small operation, a D and C, to scrape out her insides, and she'll need it now.

'Would you like the nurse to phone your husband?'

'No, thank you.'

The nurse is writing down Madeleine's details.

'Are you sure you wouldn't like me to phone? It wouldn't be any trouble.'

Madeleine's smile is polite but distant.

'No, I'll phone him in the morning. He's got a lot on his mind right now.'

Lindy stands in their lounge room this cold Sunday morning in August, looking from a distraught John to a stony-faced Madeleine. She knows nothing is going to change her friend's mind. John is on the floor, his back resting against a lounge chair. He is doubled over, clutching his knees so tightly his fingers are twisted, the knuckles bulging. Across the room, Madeleine sits bolt upright. Her hands are together in her lap, her gaze fixed on the opposite wall.

'Is it today the boys were going to Judith's?' Lindy asks, not sure who she's talking to.

Madeleine nods.

'When are they coming back?'

Madeleine mouths the words 'in the morning'.

Lindy addresses herself to John.

'I'd suggest you do as she asks, John. Staying can only make matters worse.'

He sobs and looks at his wife.

'Please, please, Madeleine, won't you at least reconsider?'

She doesn't trust herself to speak. To open her mouth would mean debating the point. The more he carries on, the more remote he becomes to her.

John has already packed a bag. He's collected his shaving gear and shoved a few clothes into the suitcase, hoping she'll relent when she realises that he might actually leave. Slowly he rises to his feet, picks up the suitcase and his car keys. The thought of living with his mother again makes him drag his heels. How long will it be before he can come back here? She sits there like a block of ice. He hits out, his lips curling back in an ugly sneer.

'You . . . you schizoid maniac . . . bitch.'

Lindy is shocked. 'Oh, John, no . . .'

Madeleine doesn't even raise her eyes.

She moves through that day like a tornado; cleaning out the kitchen cupboards, washing curtains, scrubbing floors, vacuuming the carpet, singing as she works. It's late afternoon before she can face walking into the bedroom, a pile of clean linen in her arms. There's something poking out from behind the wardrobe. Jean's painting. She'd forgotten all about it. So that's where John hid it! It must have slid sideways when he was rummaging around in the wardrobe this morning.

Near the window, she holds the rough square of board up to the light. Where is the whirlpool she saw that first time? What about those swirls of colour? These moving lines are just thick ridges of badly applied paint. Were those paint-brush hairs there before?

Madeleine holds the painting against her chest and sighs. 'Oh, Jean,' she whispers softly.

There's a packet of green plastic bags in the laundry. She pulls off the top one, shakes it once or twice, shoves the painting inside and ties two corners of the bag into a loose knot. The garbage bin is at the side of the house. Madeleine lifts the lid and pushes the green plastic parcel down one side. She stands there feeling as if she's at a funeral, biting her lip, refusing to cry. Then she slams down the garbage lid and hurries inside.

In the bathroom she empties the contents of several bottles into a saucepan – Valium, Librium, Serepax, Cogentin. There's another three bottles of Lithium still left in the kitchen cupboard. In they go as well. She adds a pint of water and stirs the lot into a thick gooey mess on the stove.

Cheerfully, humming a marching song she remembers from school, Madeleine carries the saucepan out to the toilet and upends it into the sani-pan.

To hell with the lot of them! She's never going to take another mind-numbing tablet ever again.

She cooks a cake to celebrate, and makes some chocolate crackles. Michael's eyes will widen when he sees those. Now, what will she have for tea? Toast and honey? What a relief not having to cook a big meal! She munches toast and writes herself notes, tots up figures on a scrap of paper. The car won't pass rego with that baldy back tyre, and the engine's got a knock in it. Where will she get the money to pay for it all?

Gerry at the RSL is high on her list of priorities. First thing Monday morning she's on the phone explaining her situation. Without child care there's no way she can continue with the job. He promises to send a good reference in the mail.

She dials another number. The woman she speaks to is helpful. Madeleine would be entitled to go on the pension after six months, but in the mean time, if she can get a letter from her psychiatrist, she'll probably be eligible for sickness benefits.

Another scrap of paper, another lot of figures. She's got $300 saved, but that won't be enough. Maybe Lindy and Dick would act as guarantors for her? She rummages around in John's drawers, searching for the car's registration papers.

....

Bob Dixon is a likeable bloke. His uncle began the business thirty years ago, bless him, but Bob's the man in charge at Dixon Motors now. He's built up a reputation. Honest Bob, they call him. If he can do you a good turn he will. That's what he tells the widow, Mrs Roberts, when she comes asking his advice.

'He knew the car wasn't worth much,' says Madeleine, 'but he wanted to make sure I could sell it without any hassle.'

'And that's his signature?' Bob asks, taking the document from her hand.

'Yes. He was very sick, so it's a bit wobbly. What do you think the car's worth, Mr Dixon?'

Bob walks around the VW, opens the two doors, runs his hand along the roof edge. The paintwork is good, except for the roof, which has been affected by the sun. He could probably sell it at auction – some young fellows like doing these up. Mmm, that tyre is a problem. What mileage has it done?

He straightens up and shifts his glance to the rows of cars in the yard.

'Trouble is, I've not really got anything on the lot right now to offer you . . .' He gives her a long look and winks at her little boy. Poor bugger. It must be hard. His mother raised three boys on her own, and she grew old long before her time.

'I'll tell you what I'll do . . .'

There's a car he knows about, a 1960 model Chrysler Valiant. It used to belong to a local butcher. The upholstery is in perfect condition, and the motor runs like a charm. It's a bargain at $750. He could have it here on Thursday.

'And what can you offer me on this?'

Madeleine pats the bonnet.

'How about you check out the Valiant, and if you like it I'll offer you $350 for yours. I won't make any money out of the deal, but I want to help. Sound OK?'

'Oh yes, you've been a big help. Thank you so much. See you on Thursday, Mr Dixon.'

Later, back home again, Madeleine runs up the street with Michael and Christopher like a young girl. She's got the form from the bank, and she's taking it to Lindy's place for Dick to sign. While she's there, she'll ask him what a 1960 model Valiant looks like.

Mr Dixon was right. The upholstery is in perfect condition. It's blue leather; the colour matches the carpet and the padded inserts on each door. There are pull-down armrests in the front and the back. Christopher insists that the front one is his seat. He wants to sit in the middle, next to Madeleine. Michael kneels next to him, looking out the window. She hasn't driven an automatic before. This one has five metal buttons protruding from the dashboard on the right-hand side of the steering wheel. A push-button automatic – what a thrill! The only problem is petrol. Valiants guzzle the stuff. Madeleine will soon tell anyone who asks, it's built like a tank, drinks like a fish and kicks like a mule.

Owning the car is important. She did the wheeling and dealing, she paid for it – with a little help from the bank – and now it's hers. There's something symbolic about that ritzy old grey relic. It's her mobility, her independence. It proves she can manage on her own.

John drives past at odd hours. There's no sign of anyone, no strange car in the driveway, but she's cunning. She thinks she can fool him, but he just has to be patient. He'll find out who's giving her all this dough.

Madeleine is finding it hard to manage. The only thing she can cut down on is food. She eats sparingly, particularly every second weekend, when the boys are with their father. She doesn't mind; every little helps.

One Saturday morning she drives down the hill to Green Valley, to the Sydney City Mission. A volunteer, Lou Chaney, takes the time to talk to her, and they have a cup of tea. Afterwards he carries a small cardboard box packed with groceries out to her car.

'How long have you owned this little beauty?' he asks, casting an appreciative eye over the Valiant.

'Not long. It's expensive to run, though. I suppose I should sell it . . .'

'Don't do that, my girl. You hang on to it. When you live this far out you need transport.'

He props the box between his stomach and the car, waiting while she unlocks the front passenger door. Madeleine stands back, and Lou puts the cardboard box on the seat.

She unpacks the box on the kitchen table. The brown paper bag contains tea leaves – about a third of a half-pound packet, she'd guess. Four ounces of butter, a small amount of sugar and two tins of tomato soup. She reads the label on the third tin. Asparagus tips. Madeleine drops the tin back into the cardboard box and bursts into tears.

It's a warm Christmas morning. John arrives at the house early. Madeleine and her Aunt Thelma are sitting at the kitchen table, sipping cups of coffee. The boys are still in their pyjamas, running up and down the hallway and shrieking with excitement. Toys and torn pieces of discarded wrapping paper are scattered around the floor beneath the Christmas tree, and the house is filled with the smell of dinner cooking in the oven. John has such a huge pile of presents in his arms that he can't see over the top.

'Daddy, Daddy, look what I got,' Christopher cries, shoving an Action Man doll against his father's legs.

'I got a garage, Dad, see . . .' Michael points to a brightly painted toy garage surrounded by several Matchbox cars.

'. . . and this car's a Valiant,' he adds proudly, holding up a grey car still in its box.

John puts down his parcels and has a closer look.

'No, that's a Chevvy, Michael.'

'No, it's not. Mummy said it's just like hers, didn't you, Mum?'

Thelma hurries over to give John a welcoming kiss on the cheek.

'Would you like a cup of coffee, John?'

'Yeah, Thelma. Thanks.'

'Sit down,' Madeleine says with a wary smile.

'No, thanks, I'll sit here on the floor with the kids. Do you want to open your presents, boys?'

The boys make a beeline for the gaily wrapped parcels.

Madeleine busies herself with the discarded wrapping paper. Some of the bigger pieces she folds and sets to one side; the rest go into the plastic garbage bag. When the excitement levels drop a little, she dresses first Michael then Christopher. Thelma bastes the turkey and washes up the breakfast dishes. John assembles the mechanical train and then begins sorting sections of racing-car track.

'Do you like the things I bought them?' he asks.

Surprised at the question, Madeleine moves closer to admire the array of toys. There's a jigsaw with twelve giant-sized pieces, several picture books, a remote-controlled car, a kite still in its cellophane packet, a brightly coloured record player with three child-proof records that play nursery rhymes, a box of wooden bricks and an electronic kit in a ready-to-use box. John picks up the kit and hands it to her.

'They can make a crystal radio or a doorbell with that.'

Madeleine puts the kit back on the floor. The cricket bat is probably too big for Michael, and she's not sure that ball wouldn't crack his head open. Does she dare ask John to keep the football at his place? Why couldn't he have bought a few clothes instead of some of these things?

'You must have spent a lot of money, John.'

His chin tilts defiantly.

'Funny, I was just thinking that about your presents.'

'Father Christmas, you mean, don't you?' asks Madeleine in a hoarse whisper. What is he on about?

Michael and Christopher are playing over near the front door. There's a lot of noise and laughter.

'I didn't spend much money, John – I haven't got it to spend. Take a good look at these things. I can tell you what each of them cost, if you like.'

He points a section of track at her chest.

'Don't think I can't work it out. I know you're getting help from some bloke. Do you really think I'm blind?'

'It's Christmas day. Think of the boys,' Thelma pleads, looking directly at John.

'No. No. It's all right, Aunt.'

Madeleine sits down in a chair facing John.

'You really want to know where I got the money?'

'Yes, that bloody car must've cost a bit and . . . and you've bought all the trimmings for dinner, I'll bet.'

'I didn't want the boys to miss out. Would you rather I neglected them?'

'Who is he? Do I know him?'

She feels a mixture of pity and frustration. She is tempted to tell him about the pass Keith made when she was filling the car with petrol last week, and how Cora Brent's husband eyed her off in the supermarket a while back. If she'd wanted any old man . . .

'I surrendered your life insurance policy. You might remember I was paying it out of the child endowment each quarter. The policy might've been on your life, John, but it was in my name. The amount was $1297. Would you like to see the receipt?'

He stares at her, dumb with disbelief.

Madeleine continues. 'I took out a small bank loan for the car and paid it up last month. Ask Lindy and Dick if you don't believe me. It was Dick who went guarantor for me.'

He whispers softly, 'You bloody bitch.'

Her laugh is bitter and brief. 'I can't win, can I? You'd much rather hear that I was having an affair, but you know I'm telling the truth, so you have to find something . . .'

'I've had enough of this.'

John jumps up from the floor. Madeleine winces when the front door slams.

Michael is tearful.

'I can't play with my racing set now.'

She strokes his arm.

'Never mind, the instruction booklet is right here. I'll read it first, then we'll do it together. Auntie Thelma will help, won't you, Auntie?'

'Of course, love, of course.'

. . . .

Madeleine throws back the covers and jumps out of bed. Who could be phoning at this hour? She darts down the hallway. John's voice comes screaming down the line. His speech sounds slurred, and she can't make out what he's saying at first.

What's the time? She checks the kitchen clock. Ten minutes past five. She waits for him to draw breath.

'Have you any idea what time it is, John?'

'Why should I care? You've wrecked my life, you bloody

bitch. I can't even get an insurance policy now. You know I'm a diabetic. You did this on purpose . . .'

'I did it because *I* needed money. Don't you remember I phoned you and asked if we could talk about what I should do? You hung up, do you remember, John . . .'

'I didn't know you were going to do this, did I?'

She holds the receiver away from her ear. What's the use? She waits.

'Are you still there, Madeleine? Are you listening to me?'

'I'm here.'

'Why? Tell me why you've done this to me. I loved you, I did everything for you and the kids, everything. Why?'

'Like you said, John, I'm a bitch.'

There's an abrupt click. He's gone. She replaces the receiver and hurries into her bedroom to get dressed. Minutes later, she's out the back door, down the steps and around the side of the house, opening up the gates.

It's a fair distance from the end of the yard to the front lawn, but she works tirelessly, carrying one cement pot at a time. Some of the bigger ones are really heavy too. She makes one hundred and forty-five trips.

Eventually all the orchids are lined up on the front lawn. Madeleine counts them one last time. She can hear a lawn mower. Ah, time for the town crier bit! Up and down her street she runs, yelling out to the neighbours. She's got orchids to give away, come and get 'em, tomorrow will be too late.

They are hesitant at first.

'Are you sure?'

'Don't you want some money for them?'

She is gleefully insistent. 'I'm sure, I'm sure. No, no money, they're yours.'

Peter lives next door. She pushes a big pot into his hands. He walks away quickly, half-expecting her to change her mind. Soon there's a queue. Madeleine is in a jovial mood, and the atmosphere around her is charged with good humour. Neighbours gather in twos and threes, sharing a joke, talking like old friends. How did Christmas go? Too much to eat and drink as usual? Me too. They are reluctant to leave, but the house is in a mess and they've got visitors coming. See you later. We must have a drink soon. I'll take you up on that.

A station wagon pulls into the kerb. There is something vaguely familiar about the driver. He says hello and explains that he lives in the next street.

'Of course,' says Madeleine, 'I've seen you over the fence.'

He walks around the back of the car.

'I hear you're moving.'

'You could say that. Have you come for these?'

She points at the row of remaining orchids. Forty-five, to be exact.

'Are you moving into a flat or something?' he asks, puzzled by her generosity. These orchids are worth a few bob.

'Yeah, that's right,' she replies, keen to put his mind at rest.

She helps him load the back of his car.

'This is very kind of you.'

'No, not me, my husband. They were his . . .'

She lifts another pot onto the tailboard.

'. . . you could say he's made a lot of people happy.'

'Too bloody right,' the man agrees. Wait till he tells his wife. Ten whopping big orchids for nothing. Aren't some people wonderful? It's enough to restore your faith in human nature.

Madeleine sits on the front steps. The orchids are all gone. Every last one of them. She feels as if an enormous weight has been lifted from her shoulders.

Thelma's smile is tinged with concern. She hopes Madeleine knows what she's doing.

'You've had a busy morning, love. Fancy a cold turkey sandwich?'

The boys run up the street ahead of their mother.

'Stay on the footpath, Christopher,' she calls out.

In the gate and up the steps. Lindy greets them at the door.

'Have you got time for a coffee before you go?' she asks Madeleine.

'Sure. Shall we get these two into bed first?'

'OK. Well, let me do that. You put the kettle on. Come on, fellows. Give your mum a kiss goodnight.'

Lindy sips her coffee. She has a mischievous gleam in her eye.

'So what's it like to be orchid-free?'

Madeleine pulls a face before replying.

'Amazing. I still can't believe I did it.'

'Does John know?'

'Not yet.'

Lindy puts down her mug and turns to the stove. She lights the gas under a saucepan.

'Did you hear about Cora Brent?'

'No. Who's she picking on this week?'

Lindy grins at Madeleine, but says nothing. She is savouring the moment.

Madeleine rises out of her chair.

'Come on, tell me.'

'She's been charged with assault.'

Madeleine's eyes widen in surprise.

'Who? What? I mean who . . .'

'She attacked Mr Glover.'

'Mr Glover? Who's he?'

'You know, the estate agent.'

'Oh, him. But why?'

'Apparently he warned her not to bother him again or he'd get the police on to her. She must've done her lolly. Ellie from over the back – you know, the one who lives in that big house on the corner? – well, I saw her in the garage this afternoon. She said Cora ran amok with a hammer.'

'My God, she could've killed him.'

'Nah, I think she only managed a couple of blows. Mind you, he's probably got a bad headache right now.'

Madeleine is staring at her empty mug.

'Fancy that. So if I'm mad, what's she?'

'And that's not all. Her husband is threatening to leave her.'

'How do you know that?'

Lindy stirs the contents of the saucepan.

'The whole street knows. While you were out this afternoon they had a row. It was after she came back from the police station. He was yelling and carrying on.'

'She must be in a bad way.'

Lindy nods in agreement. 'She has had a lot to put up with.'

Madeleine looks up at the kitchen clock.

'I'd better go. Dick will be home soon, won't he?'

'Yeah, any minute now.'

Lindy turns the gas down and follows Madeleine to the front door.

'You know, I wanted to ask you something . . .'

'Yeah, what?' Madeleine says.

'I suppose it's Cora that's made me think about all this, but do you think it was your marriage that caused your breakdown?'

Madeleine takes her time answering.

'No, I don't. It wasn't a good relationship – I'm not sure if it ever was. I don't hate him or anything, but I did have to make changes, and he didn't seem to want that . . .'

'It makes you realise nothing is certain, doesn't it?'

'True. Nothing is. I'm sorry to cut this short, love, but I really must go.'

'Of course. Have a good meeting.'

....

Madeleine opens up the door and switches on the light. The hall smells of cigarette smoke. She sets about opening windows. Carole and Daphne walk in together. David is next. He hurries over to help Madeleine. She climbs down from the chair to let him take her place.

'Thanks,' she says. 'Those last two are quite high, aren't they?'

'My pleasure. Besides, you can't be expected to do everything.'

She laughs, unable to think of a suitable reply.

The youngest member of the group, Katrina Ezzy, arrives an hour late. She seems nervous and fidgety, but says nothing.

Someone asks why Barbara isn't here tonight.

'Her sister says she was admitted to Rydalmere last Sunday,' Madeleine reports.

'Did she say why?' David asks.

Madeleine pauses briefly before answering him.

'She tried to kill herself.'

'Why didn't she phone one of us if she felt desperate?' Carole wonders.

'You lot!' Katrina jumps up and stands on her chair. 'You act like you know everything!'

No one speaks. David turns a worried face towards Madeleine. They're all waiting to see what she will do.

'Say what you want to say, Katrina.'

'Oh, listen to her, Madame Social Worker . . .' Hands on hips, Katrina rolls her eyes and assumes an accent.

'Say what you want to say, Katrina.'

Hazel is indignant. 'Maybe you should go home till you can behave yourself, Katrina.'

'No!' Madeleine says.

Her tone takes them all by surprise.

'I'm sorry if I offended you, Hazel,' she continues, 'but the whole idea of self-help is to try and understand each other.'

'Sorry,' Hazel mumbles, slumping down in her seat.

Madeleine's hands are under the table. She presses her fingers hard against the wooden edge underneath. Silently she begs Katrina to talk about what's upsetting her.

Maria can't stand silence. She gets up and walks over to the kitchen area. They can hear her clinking cups, putting things on a tray. David coughs. Hazel looks close to tears. Madeleine maintains her silence. Katrina gets down off her chair and slips out the door. Madeleine makes no effort to call her back. The meeting resumes.

Madeleine answers a knock at the door. Katrina is on the doorstep. She is not alone. Father Patrick, the new parish priest, is with her.

'Katrina asked me to come, Madeleine. Is this a convenient time?'

Katrina has been in and out of hospital for the past six years. That's a lot of years when you're only twenty. Now they want to put her back again.

'I reckon the doctor and me mother are in cahoots,' Katrina says. 'They reckon I'm a danger to myself, but what they really mean is I'm a nuisance.'

Father Patrick raises his palm. He wants to get a word in.

'Katrina thinks you can help her, Madeleine. Can you?'

'I don't know. I'm not as experienced as some of the other SHEPP people, but I might be able to help.'

'Is there anyone who could vouch for your behaviour?' Father Patrick asks Katrina. 'I mean someone who could put another point of view . . .'

'No one they'd listen to . . . they . . .'

Madeleine interrupts. 'What do *you* think should happen, Katrina?'

A crooked smile teases the corners of Katrina's mouth.

'They've been saying a lot of things about me. I think I should uncover their little game.'

Madeleine has no idea what Katrina is talking about, but she smiles at the girl encouragingly. There's something about Katrina she can't help liking. She has spirit and a sense of humour.

'Perhaps we could discuss what you might say to your doctor? And maybe Father Patrick would be willing to talk to your mother?'

'Yes, I'd be happy to do that,' Father Patrick says.

Katrina yawns and looks bored. 'Talk, talk, that's all you people ever want to do.'

Two days later Katrina is back. This time she's alone. She has a plan. She wants to infiltrate the hospital and get hold of her file. And she wants Madeleine's help.

'I've already pinched a nurse's uniform, and I know exactly what to do, but I need someone to drive me there and back . . .' – that same crooked smile – '. . . like in the movies, you know, the getaway car? Will you do it?'

Madeleine wants to say no. She's scared, but she can't let Katrina know that. She stalls by asking a number of questions.

'What if you're caught? Won't they recognise you? What would they do to us?'

Katrina has the upper hand. She knows Madeleine is tempted. Step by step, she goes through the plan again. She's thought about nothing else for days. She can do it. They can do it together.

Madeleine is about to say no, but Katrina gets in first.

'I dare you.'

I dare you. I dare you. I double dare you. Fraidy cat, fraidy cat, too scared to get off the mat. For a brief moment Madeleine is ten years old, listening to Tim and Lizzie daring her to walk along the edge of the front fence, to run into the flats across the road and push a tiny piece of coal into the shiny silver top of a neighbour's milk bottle, to climb the steps to the reservoir at the top of their street in Bondi Junction and prick her finger with a piece of the rolled-up barbed wire that blocks the steps halfway up. Madeleine was told a child had drowned in that reservoir. She didn't know when it was, but in the moments before sleep each night she saw that little girl, floating face-down on the top of the water.

How did she ever manage to climb those steps with her legs shaking so badly? She could hear that little girl calling, pleading with her to come and save her. I dare you, I dare you. Three magic words. Up she went, despite her fear, keen to prove she was no coward.

'OK, Katrina, you're on. When?'

On Wednesday Madeleine drives the boys to school. Michael runs off to join his friends while she walks to the gate with Christopher. He blows her a kiss when he gets to the class-room door. Katrina is waiting around the corner. She's wearing a blue uniform. Her hair is swept back under the cap. She's even got the right shoes.

Madeleine pushes open the passenger door.

'The size of your uniform is perfect, Katrina. How did you manage that?'

Katrina hops in and shoves a plastic bag on the floor.

'I did my research.'

Madeleine checks her rear-vision mirror and eases the car out from the kerb.

'Yes, but you could hardly have pinched it off a nurse's back. Where did you get it?'

Katrina undoes the lace on one shoe and wiggles her white-stockinged toes.

'The hospital laundry. The thing about these places is that one department never knows what another department's doing. You can pretend to be anyone. How would they know?'

She slips her shoe back on and does up the lace.

'These bloody things are killin' me.'

'And where did they come from?'

'St Vincent de Paul. What do you think I am, a bloody thief?'

Madeleine turns right into Victoria Road, then left into the hospital grounds. There's a small carpark near the kiosk. They've agreed she'll wait there.

Katrina rifles through the plastic bag and pulls out a glasses case. The wire-rimmed spectacles make her look older and prissy. She turns her head so that Madeleine can judge the effect.

'Do they suit me?'

Madeleine is breaking out in a sweat. This is a stupid idea. Get in the car, Katrina. Let's get out of this place. But it's too late now.

'Are we talking fashion here or disguise?'

'Disguise, naturally.'

'They're wonderful, but can you see out of them?'

'Just. They're my sister's.'

'You mean you're wearing your sister's glasses and she doesn't know? Has she got another pair?'

'You really do sound awfully boring sometimes. Who cares, anyway? If you met my sister you'd feel sorry for me.'

'Right now, Miss Ezzy, I feel sorry for *me*.'

Katrina is getting out of the car. 'I'll be back before you know it.'

'You'd better be. Good luck.'

Katrina walks away briskly, straight up to the administration block.

The clerk behind the counter is friendly. She greets the nurse with a comment about the weather.

'Nice to see the sun for a change.'

'Sure is,' replies Katrina. 'They keepin' you busy?'

'Flat to the boards. What about you?'

'Yeah, Ward 5 is hectic as per usual. We got a coupla new admissions . . .'

'New or old?' the clerk asks obligingly.

'They've been here before. Let me get my bit of paper.'

Katrina makes a show of drawing the slip of paper from her pocket. She reads out: 'Surname Ezzy, first name Katrina. Dr Kemble told me the address as well. Do you need that too?'

'No, not unless they're being transferred from somewhere else.'

The clerk jots down the details.

'I always have to write things down. My head's like a sieve.'

'Here, take this,' says Katrina, handing over her slip of paper.

'Thanks. Shall I send these over?'

Katrina has prepared herself for this moment.

'No, I have to wait. Dr Kemble is in one helluva mood this morning. He said I had to get them to him pronto.'

The clerk isn't happy.

'These doctors think they're gods. Does he realise how many files I've got to go through?'

Katrina leans on the counter.

'Knowing him, he probably wouldn't give a damn,' she says companionably.

Madeleine's right leg is trembling. She has hit her knee on the steering-wheel twice. Where the hell is Katrina? She shouldn't have been this long. A nurse walks past the kiosk. It's Quigley. Madeleine slides down in her seat. She squeezes her toes hard against the floor in an attempt to keep her legs still. Her knee immediately shoots out to the side and bangs against the car door. Ow.

She raises herself to peep out the side window. Nurse Quigley has walked on, Madeleine can see her back retreating into the distance. Should she start the motor? But that might attract attention. What is that girl *doing*?

Katrina pulls open the door.

'Hurry, Madeleine, get us out of here.'

'Don't worry, I will.'

The Valiant thrums into life. Madeleine touches the accelerator pedal lightly. She's bothered about her leg. It has to settle down soon.

Katrina says nothing till they're out the gate.

'I got it, I got it.'

'Bloody hell,' says Madeleine, 'that file is as thick as an encyclopedia. But you've got two. Don't tell me your file is in two volumes?'

Katrina places a thick book-like file on the pull-down armrest.

'No, this one is yours. Think of it as a present.'

Also by Wakefield Press

RAGE OF ANGELS
Barry Westburg

Rage of Angels juxtaposes weirdly comic scenes from the several lives of Rick Richards, expatriate Yank, and other maimed menfolk and wounded women who have become lost in space, unzipped in time. Sometimes real life – with its cornshuckings, rusted Mustangs, haunted Rhineland castles, surfing sergeants, violated villas, Asian chicken shops, piping shrikes, IVF clinics and water babies – can dissolve into a cartoon Western or a road movie. And almost always does.

'Barry Westburg's short stories are fantasies of another order – American Midwestern noir, Australian suburban dreaming, hilarious memoirs, enigmatic fables, literary theory games and surreal satire.'
– Michael Sharkey, The *Australian*

ISBN 1 86254 448 4   RRP $19.95

Also by Wakefield Press

ONE FOR THE MASTER

Dorothy Johnston

When Helen Plathe sets out along the Barwon River path for her first day at Highlands woollen mill, she is following in the footsteps of her mother, her uncle and her grandmother. Inside Highlands' tall black gates, Helen is initiated into an extraordinary world and discovers its secret history.

Like a medieval castle, the bluestone tower of Highlands casts a long shadow over those who work there – the maverick Queenie Bisset, railing against a world of men who 'liked neat ideas, and liked their women to be neat as well'; Helen's uncle, Lennie Pritchard, tragically thwarted in his bid to make a new life outside the mill; young Wally Sullivan, torn between his family and his struggle to keep the mill afloat; and the mysterious Miss Foot, silent witness to the decline of an industry that has ruled the lives of the people along the river from generation to generation.

ISBN 1 86254 408 5   RRP $19.95

Also by Wakefield Press

SLOW BOAT TO MONGOLIA
Lydia Laube

Who else but Lydia Laube would climb the Great Wall of China waving a pink parasol while riding a donkey? In *Slow Boat to Mongolia* Lydia tells of her travels by ship, train and bone-shaking bus through Indonesia and China on her way to fabled Outer Mongolia.

Lydia learns how to use chopsticks with aplomb and ploughs her way through crowds to visit places few westerners have ever seen. She reaches Outer Mongolia, where she stays in a *ger* in the snow and rides a horse through waist-high silvery grass.

The intrepid author of *Behind the Veil* and *The Long Way Home* returns with her most adventurous tale yet.

ISBN 1 86254 418 2   RRP $16.95

ON MY BROTHERS' SHOULDERS
Ty André with Allen McMahon

'A story of remarkable achievement.' Jack Thompson

One evening in 1952, a young woman walked down to the Mekong River carrying her baby boy in a home-made basket. She lit a candle and stood it in the basket, then set her baby adrift on the stream.

Miraculously the child was rescued by a fisherman and taken to a Catholic mission on the island of Cu Lao Gieng. The little boy was named 'Ty', meaning 'billion', because the odds against his survival were a billion to one.

This is a story of that one-in-a-billion chance. For six long years Ty lived with hunger and pain. His arms and legs were crippled by polio, and he was so starved of human company that he did not know his own name. Then a young man who was visiting the mission caught sight of the tiny youngster wriggling along the ground to take a drink at the river. From that chance encounter was born a relationship that would transform both their lives, and a personal crusade that would give hope to thousands of other children in war-torn Vietnam.

ISBN 1 86254 378 X   RRP $19.95

Also by Wakefield Press

EYE OF THE WHITE HAWK
Stories by Bary Dowling

In *Eye of the White Hawk* Bary Dowling tells stories rich in
their evocation of a world close to nature. Set in the city, or
rural Australia, or the bush, these are stories of interior
lives, and of transformations achieved through effort, seeking
and discovery, a process that never stops.

'A special virtuosity that brings us back with a jolt to believe
the centre of the world is not urban, or suburban, but in the
silences of our own landscape. Dowling strikes gold.'

—Thomas Shapcott

ISBN 1 86254 421 2   RRP $17.95

Also by Wakefield Press

SENTENCE: SIBERIA
A story of survival

Ann Lehtmets and Douglas Hoile

Ann Lehtmets is one of few women in the western world to have lived through Stalin's holocaust.

One morning in June 1941, Russian soldiers arrested Ann Lehtmets in her home in Estonia, tore her from her husband and children and loaded her in a cattle truck, destination unknown.

She survived her sentence in Siberia, negotiating a life where secret police, brutish foremen and hostile landladies conspired with cold, hunger and backbreaking labour to make existence difficult for all and deadly for many.

Ann Lehtmets owes her life to spirit, intelligence, guile and humour. These qualities shine through every page of her extraordinary recollections.

ISBN 1 86254 313 5   RRP $18.95

Wakefield Press has been publishing good Australian books
for over fifty years. For a catalogue of current and
forthcoming titles, or to add your name to our mailing list,
send your name and address to

Wakefield Press, Box 2266, Kent Town, South Australia 5071.

TELEPHONE (08) 8362 8800 FAX (08) 8362 7592
WEB www.wakefieldpress.com.au